CALIFORNIA

McDougal Littell

MATH
Algebra 1

Larson Boswell Kanold Stiff

Practice Workbook

The Practice Workbook provides additional practice for every lesson in the textbook. The workbook covers essential skills as well as problem solving. Space is provided for students to show their work. Answers to the Practice Workbook exercises are provided on the interleaf pages of the Teacher's Edition and in the Chapter Resource Books.

McDougal Littell
A DIVISION OF HOUGHTON MIFFLIN COMPANY
Evanston, Illinois • Boston • Dallas

ISBN 13: 978-0-618-89302-7
ISBN 10: 0-618-89302-4

3456789–DEI–14 13 12 11 10 09 08

Contents

Chapter

Program Overview

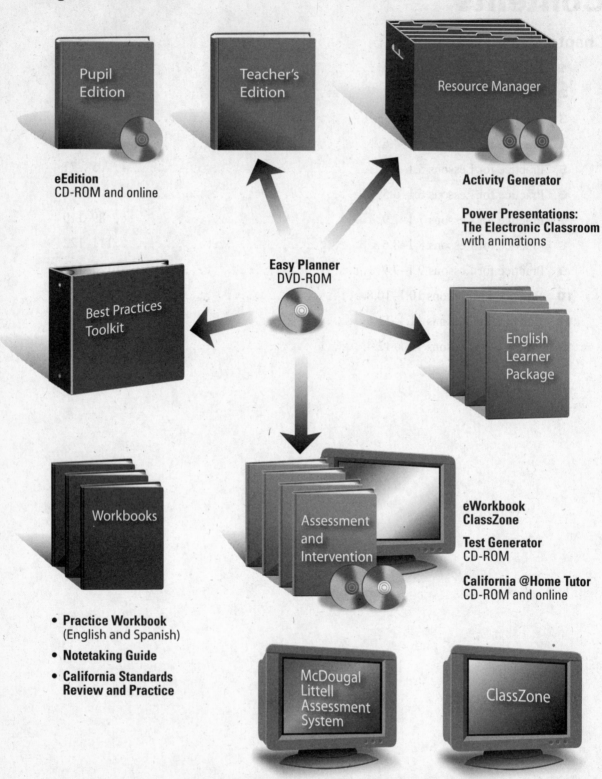

Pupil Edition

eEdition
CD-ROM and online

Teacher's Edition

Resource Manager

Activity Generator

**Power Presentations:
The Electronic Classroom**
with animations

Best Practices Toolkit

Easy Planner
DVD-ROM

English Learner Package

Workbooks

- **Practice Workbook**
  (English and Spanish)
- **Notetaking Guide**
- **California Standards
  Review and Practice**

Assessment and Intervention

**eWorkbook
ClassZone**

Test Generator
CD-ROM

California @Home Tutor
CD-ROM and online

McDougal Littell Assessment System

ClassZone

Practice Workbook Overview

The Practice Workbook provides
additional practice for the lessons
in the textbook that includes:

- Skill practice
- Problem solving practice
- Space for students to show their work

LESSON
1.1 **Practice**
For use with pages 5–10

CA Standards
Gr. 6 AF 1.2

Evaluate the expression.

1. $y + 12$ when $y = 29$ **2.** $47 - x$ when $x = 38$ **3.** $0.8a$ when $a = 7.5$

4. $12.5 + m$ when $m = 7.6$ **5.** $r(4.6)$ when $r = 8.1$ **6.** $6.25 \div g$ when $g = 2.5$

7. $\dfrac{x}{0.9}$ when $x = 54$ **8.** $\dfrac{62}{d}$ when $d = 3.1$ **9.** $\dfrac{4}{7} \cdot t$ when $t = \dfrac{7}{8}$

10. $r(8.3)$ when $r = 10.2$ **11.** $w + \dfrac{2}{5}$ when $w = \dfrac{1}{2}$ **12.** $\dfrac{n}{2.4}$ when $n = 12$

Write the power in words and as a product.

13. 8^7 **14.** $(0.1)^4$ **15.** x^5

Evaluate the power.

16. 9^2 **17.** 2^6 **18.** $(0.4)^3$

Evaluate the expression.

19. x^2 when $x = \dfrac{1}{5}$ **20.** m^4 when $m = 0.6$ **21.** $2y^3$ when $y = 4$

LESSON 1.1

Practice *continued*
For use with pages 5–10

22. Side Table A side table has interior storage space in the shape of a cube. What is the volume of the storage space if the interior length is 12 inches?

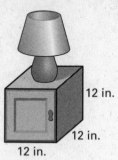

12 in.

12 in.

12 in.

23. Playing Cards There are 52 cards in a standard deck of playing cards. You are combining decks of cards so that you can play a game with a large number of people. The expression 52d represents the number of cards in d decks. If you combine 4 decks of cards, how many cards will you have altogether?

24. Sales Tax An item costs c dollars and 6% sales tax is charged. The total cost including sales tax is given by the expression 1.06c. You are buying a skateboard that costs $75. What is the cost of the skateboard including sales tax?

25. Flower Arranging You are creating a flower arrangement for a friend. The total cost (in dollars) for one vase and f flowers is given by the expression $8 + 2.5f$. How much will it cost to make an arrangement with 8 flowers?

Name _____   Date _____

Practice
For use with pages 11–17

Evaluate the expression.

1. $16 \div 8 \cdot 5$

2. $7^2 - 24 \div 3$

3. $5 + 1.2 \div 0.3$

4. $18 \div 6 + 4 \cdot 3$

5. $13 - 15 \div 5 + 9$

6. $\frac{2}{3} \cdot 3^2 - 5$

7. $8(6 - 2) + 4$

8. $28 - 3(4 + 5)$

9. $1.2 \cdot 5 - 6 \div 3$

10. $(11 + 15) \div 13$

11. $35 - 3^2 \cdot 2$

12. $\frac{4}{5}(3 \cdot 20) - 17$

Evaluate the expression.

13. $3x^4 - 5$ when $x = 5$

14. $8m^3 \div 6$ when $m = 3$

15. $200 - 3y^2$ when $y = 8$

16. $5c^2 - 2c$ when $c = 9$

17. $3 \cdot 18t^2$ when $t = \frac{1}{3}$

18. $\frac{42}{n} + n$ when $n = 6$

19. $\frac{5a}{b - 6}$ when $a = 8$ and $b = 12$

20. $\frac{4d^2}{c} + 3$ when $c = 6$ and $d = 3$

21. Was the expression evaluated correctly using the order of operations? If not, find and correct the error.

$$80 - \frac{1}{3}(15)^2 = 80 - 5^2 = 80 - 25 = 55$$

LESSON 1.2 **Practice** *continued*
For use with pages 11–17

22. Tournament During a bowling tournament, you bowled three games with scores of 110, 130, and 129, respectively. Your average bowling score is given by $\frac{110 + 130 + 129}{3}$. What is your average score?

23. Painting Three weeks ago, an art supply store started selling a paint kit for 75% of the original price. Now the kit is 15% off of the sale price. The expression $0.75x - 0.15(0.75x)$ represents the current price of the paint kit where x is the kit's original price (in dollars). Find the current price of the kit if it originally cost $48.

24. Crown Molding You are decorating the perimeter of the ceiling of your living room with crown molding. The expression $2x + 2y$ represents the total amount of molding you need where x is the width of the room (in feet) and y is the length of the room (in feet). Find the total amount of wood you need if the room is 11 feet wide and 10.5 feet long.

25. Core Sample Before a structure is built on a plot of land, it is sometimes necessary to test the surface beneath the plot of land to determine its integrity. So, it may be necessary to take a core sample which is cylindrical in shape. Find the volume of the core sample shown by using the expression $\pi r^2 h$ where r is the radius (in inches) and h is the height (in inches) of the cylinder. Use 3.14 for π.

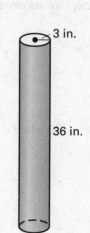

3 in.

36 in.

Practice
For use with pages 18–24

Translate the verbal phrase into an expression.

1. The difference of 9 and a number n

2. The quotient of a number y and 22

3. The sum of 57 and a number b

4. $\frac{2}{3}$ of a number x

5. 18 less than a number c

6. 25 more than twice a number m

7. The quotient of 8 and twice a number z

8. The sum of 2 and the square of a number r

Write an expression for the situation.

9. The amount of money you spent if you started with $40 and now have d dollars

10. The total height of a 1-foot tall birdbath if it is placed on a base that is b feet tall

11. Each person's share of baseball cards if 4 people share c cards equally

12. Number of minutes in h hours

Name _____   Date _____

Find the unit rate.

13. $\dfrac{\$75}{5 \text{ video games}}$ 14. $\dfrac{600 \text{ students}}{8 \text{ classes}}$ 15. $\dfrac{32 \text{ pencils}}{4 \text{ boxes}}$

16. **Candle Making** You are making candles for your friends. A mold for the candles
costs $22.50 and wax to make one candle costs $5. Write an algebraic expression for
the total cost of making *x* candles. You make 8 candles. Find the total cost.

17. **Baseball** Last season, a baseball player scored 14 runs in 18 games. This season,
the baseball player scored 12 runs in 15 games. Find the number of runs scored per
game in each season. Round your answers to the nearest hundredth. Then identify
the season in which the player scored more runs per game.

18. **Car Trip** You are getting ready to make a 640-mile car trip. In general, your car can
be driven 160 miles on 5 gallons of gasoline. How many gallons of gasoline will you
use for the trip? You started out with 4 gallons of gasoline in your car and gasoline is
$2.29 per gallon. How much money will you spend on gasoline on the trip?

19. **Plant Trellis** You are building the wood trellis shown in the
figure so that you can grow a vine up the side of your home.
Write an expression for the total number of feet of wood needed
to build the trellis. *Hint:* Write separate expressions for the
number of feet of vertical pieces needed and the number of feet
of horizontal pieces needed. Then find the total number of feet
of wood needed if the trellis is 8 feet tall and 2 feet wide.

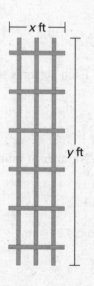

Practice
For use with pages 26–31

Write an equation or an inequality.

1. The difference of a number c and 17 is more than 33.

2. The product of 3 and a number x is at most 21.

3. The sum of 14 and twice a number y is equal to 78.

4. The difference of 22 and the quotient of a number m and 4 is 54.

5. The sum of 7 and three times a number b is at least 12.

Check whether the given number is a solution of the equation or inequality.

6. $6x + 7 = 25; 3$ **7.** $22 - 5c = 8; 3$ **8.** $\frac{b}{4} - 7 = 1; 36$

9. $7a + 4 \geq 20; 2.7$ **10.** $4y - 3 > 12; 4$ **11.** $\frac{m}{3} + 14 < 33; 9$

LESSON 1.4

Practice continued
For use with pages 26–31

Solve the equation using mental math.

12. $x + 9 = 17$ **13.** $y - 5 = 12$ **14.** $8w = 48$

15. $\dfrac{m}{4} = 16$ **16.** $2x - 1 = 15$ **17.** $3x + 2 = 20$

18. Computers You are buying a new printer and a new scanner for your computer, and you cannot spend over $150. The printer you want costs $80. Write an inequality that describes the most that you can spend on the scanner and still stay within your budget. If you buy a scanner that costs $75, will you remain within your budget?

19. Go-Carts You and three of your friends are going to race go-carts. The last time you went, you had a coupon for $3 off each admission and paid $48 for the 4 admissions. What was the total price without the coupon? You pay the regular price this time and share it equally. How much does each person pay?

20. Bracelets You are making beaded bracelets for your friends. You want to use 30 beads for each bracelet and want to use no more than 145 beads. Write an inequality that models this situation. Can you make 4 bracelets?

21. Staircase When building a staircase, you need to be concerned with the height of the riser and the depth of the tread so that people can go up and down the stairs comfortably. One rule of thumb used to determine proper riser height and tread depth is that the sum of the tread depth (in inches) and twice the riser height (in inches) should equal 26 inches. Write an equation that models this situation. The riser height of a set of steps is 5 inches. What should the depth be?

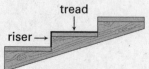

tread

riser →

California Math, Algebra 1
Chapter 1 Practice Workbook

Name _____ Date _____

In Exercises 1 and 2, identify what you know and what you need to find out. You do *not* need to solve the problem.

1. You are making cookies for a bake sale and need to make enough cookies to fill 24 boxes containing 6 cookies each. How many dozen cookies do you need to make?

2. The cellular phone plan you signed up for gives you 400 minutes a month for $35 and charges $.15 for each additional minute over 400 minutes. How long can you talk on the phone each month and stay within a budget of $45?

In Exercises 3 and 4, state the formula that is needed to solve the problem. You do *not* need to solve the problem.

3. You invest $200 into a savings account that earns 2% simple interest. How long will it take to earn $50 in interest?

4. It takes you half an hour to travel 26 miles to work. What is your average speed?

5. **Sticker Collection** Your sticker collection consists of 175 stickers. Each sticker is either an animated cartoon character or an animal. There are 42 less stickers that are animated characters than stickers that are animals. Let x be the number of stickers that are animals. Which equation correctly models this situation?

   A. $x - 42 = 175$

   B. $x + (x + 42) = 175$

   C. $x + (x - 42) = 175$

LESSON 1.5

Practice continued
For use with pages 32–37

6. Bookshelf You installed a bookshelf on the wall to organize some of your books. The books that you absolutely want on the shelf weigh a total of $6\frac{3}{4}$ pounds. The bookshelf can handle no more than 9 pounds. You plan on filling the rest of the shelf with your paperbacks that each weigh about $\frac{1}{8}$ pound. Assuming you won't run out of room, how many paperback books can you add to the shelf?

7. Camping You are responsible for buying supplies for an upcoming camping trip. You can buy packages of stew that just need water added and then are heated. Each package costs $4.95 and contains enough stew for 2 people. You need to buy enough packages so that you can have stew for 3 days of the trip. There will be 8 people on the trip. How many packages do you need? What is the total cost?

8. Banking You are going to open a certificate of deposit (CD) that earns simple interest. One bank offers a CD in which you must deposit $500 for 3 years with 2% interest. Another bank offers a CD in which you must deposit $250 for 4 years with 3% interest. Which CD will earn more interest?

Name _____ Date _____

LESSON 2.1 **Practice**
For use with pages 53–59

Graph the numbers on a number line. Then order the numbers from least to greatest.

1. $2, -3,$ and 0

$$\text{—+—+—+—+—+—+—+—+—}$$
$$-4 \ -3 \ -2 \ -1 \ \ 0 \ \ 1 \ \ 2$$

2. $-5, 7,$ and -8

$$\text{—+—+—+—+—+—+—+—+—}$$
$$-8 \quad -4 \quad 0 \quad 4 \quad 8$$

3. $-9, -12,$ and 6

$$\text{—+—+—+—+—+—+—+—}$$
$$-12 \ -9 \ -6 \ -3 \ \ 0 \ \ 3 \ \ 6$$

Tell whether each number in the list belongs to each of the following sets: whole numbers, integers, and rational numbers. Then order the numbers from least to greatest.

4. $-1.9, \dfrac{3}{4}, 0.8, -3$

5. $1.3, -2, \dfrac{1}{2}, 0$

6. $2.5, -\dfrac{7}{8}, -0.5, \dfrac{1}{3}$

For the given value of a, find $-a$ and $|a|$.

7. $a = 10.2$

8. $a = -14$

9. $a = \dfrac{1}{2}$

Identify the hypothesis and conclusion of the conditional statement. Tell whether the statement is *true* or *false*. If it is false, give a counterexample.

10. If a number is negative, then its opposite is positive.

11. If a number is even, then its opposite is a whole number.

Evaluate the expression when $x = -2.5$.

12. $-x$

13. $|x| + 3$

14. $|x| - 4$

Practice continued
For use with pages 53–69

15. Fairbanks, Alaska The table shows the monthly normal temperatures in Fairbanks, Alaska, during the winter months. Which monthly temperature is the lowest? Which months had normal temperatures below −5°F?

Month	December	January	February	March
Temperature (°F)	−7°	−10°	−4°	11°

16. Stock Market The gains and losses of a stock for a week are shown in the table. Which day showed the greatest gain? Which day showed the greatest loss?

Day	Monday	Tuesday	Wednesday	Thursday	Friday
Gain or loss	+0.02	−0.05	−0.12	−0.08	−0.01

17. Class Enrollment The table shows the growth in enrollment of the senior classes at a high school between 1999 and 2004. Which year showed the greatest increase in senior class size? Which year showed the greatest decrease in senior class size?

Year	1999	2000	2001	2002	2003	2004
Increase	15	22	−7	−12	10	18

Use a number line to find the sum.

1. $-8 + 9$

2. $13 + (-4)$

3. $-5 + (-11)$

4. $-6 + (-7)$

5. $-15 + 6$

6. $-21 + 10$

Find the sum.

7. $-4.2 + 6.5$

8. $14.2 + (-9.1)$

9. $7.8 + (-3.9)$

10. $2\frac{2}{3} + \left(-1\frac{1}{3}\right)$

11. $-7\frac{1}{2} + 10\frac{3}{4}$

12. $8\frac{2}{3} + \left(-9\frac{1}{6}\right)$

13. $-10 + (-23) + 18$

14. $-1.25 + 2.5 + 3.5$

15. $-2.6 + 7.5 + 5.6$

Evaluate the expression for the given value of x.

16. $6 + x + (-11); x = 8$

17. $-14 + x + 14; x = 9$

18. $2.2 + x + (-3.4); x = -2.5$

19. $-4.3 + (-x) + 1.5; x = 3.1$

20. $-2.8 + (-x) + 8.1; x = -3.6$

21. $-6.8 + |x| + 2.6; x = -3.2$

LESSON 2.2

Practice continued
For use with pages 60–66

Solve the equation using mental math.

22. $x + 15 + (-15) = 6$ **23.** $6 + x + (-3) = 0$ **24.** $x + (-2.5) + 6.8 = 0$

25. Delivery Driver A furniture delivery driver is given three deliveries for the morning. The first delivery is 7 miles west of the furniture store. The second delivery is 14 miles east of the first house, and the last delivery before lunch is 3 miles west of the second house. How far is the delivery driver from the store after the last delivery?

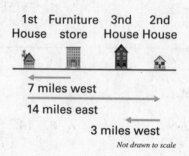

26. Homework Your history teacher gives you an extra credit question on each homework assignment. You've been keeping track of how many points you are above or below the number of regular points you can earn on each assignment. How many total points do you have if there are 125 regular homework points for the five assignments?

Assignment	1	2	3	4	5
Number of points above and below	−2	4	−1	5	−3

27. Company Profits The table shows the profits earned by a small company during the first six months of the year. Did the company make a positive profit for the first six months? If so, how much?

Month	January	February	March	April	May	June
Profit	$1500	−$2000	$1000	$3000	−$2000	−$1000

LESSON 2.2

Copyright © by McDougal Littell, a division of Houghton Mifflin Company.

LESSON 2.3 **Practice**
For use with pages 67–72

Find the difference.

1. $12 - (-7)$

2. $22 - (-28)$

3. $-6 - (-13)$

4. $-15 - (-9)$

5. $5.8 - (-7.9)$

6. $-4.1 - (-3.6)$

7. $-6.2 - (-3.6)$

8. $3.8 - (-5.9)$

9. $-2.6 - (-10.2)$

10. $\dfrac{1}{3} - \dfrac{4}{9}$

11. $\dfrac{1}{2} - \left(-\dfrac{7}{8}\right)$

12. $-\dfrac{2}{3} - \left(-\dfrac{3}{8}\right)$

Evaluate the expression when $x = -6.4$ and $y = 10.8$.

13. $y - x$

14. $x - (-y)$

15. $x - y$

16. $-y - x$

17. $x - y - 2.6$

18. $y - 5.4 - x$

19. $-7.3 - x + y$

20. $6.4 + y - x$

21. $10.8 - x - y$

22. $y - (-x) + 6.4$

23. $7.2 + y - x$

24. $4.25 - x - y$

LESSON 2.3

LESSON
2.3

Practice *continued*
For use with pages 67–72

Find the change in temperature or elevation.

25. From 15°C to −5°C

26. From −250 meters to 175 meters

27. Planet Temperatures The average temperature on the surface of Venus is 480°C and the average temperature on the surface of Mars is −65°C. How many degrees hotter is the temperature on Venus' surface than on Mars' surface?

28. Manned Submersibles Alvin, a manned submersible used in deep-sea exploration, has a maximum depth of −14,764 feet. Its first untethered dive was −35 feet. How many feet deeper is Alvin's maximum depth than the depth of its first dive?

29. Banana Prices The table shows the weekly prices (in dollars) of a pound of bananas during a month at a local supermarket. Determine the change in the price per pound each week. Find the total of these changes to determine the total change in the price per pound over the 4 weeks.

Week	1	2	3	4
Price per pound (dollars)	0.49	0.49	0.39	0.49

30. State Temperatures The table shows the record high and low temperatures for several states. Find the difference between the record high and low temperatures for each state. Which state has the greatest temperature difference?

State	Alaska	North Dakota	Wyoming	Virginia	Nevada
High temperature (°F)	100°	121°	115°	110°	125°
Low temperature (°F)	−80°	−60°	−66°	−30°	−50°

LESSON 2.3

LESSON 2.4 Practice
For use with pages 73–79

CA Standards
Alg. 1.0
Alg. 1.1

Find the product.

1. $10(-9)$

2. $-12(-3)$

3. $-11(7)$

4. $2.6(-8)$

5. $-3.2(15)$

6. $-9.5(5)$

7. $-\frac{1}{2}(28)$

8. $-\frac{2}{3}(-21)$

9. $\frac{4}{5}(-20)$

10. $-6(4)(-3.5)$

11. $-2.1(-10)(-5)$

12. $-6.5(21)(-6)$

Identify the property illustrated.

13. $5.6 \cdot (-3.2) = -3.2 \cdot 5.6$

14. $0 \cdot 2.1 = 0$

15. $-1 \cdot (-1.5) = 1.5$

Find the product. Justify your steps.

16. $-3(-5)(-4x)$

17. $-\frac{3}{4}(-20)(7y)$

18. $8x(4.2)(-5)$

Evaluate the expression when $x = -3$ and $y = 4.1$.

19. $x + 2y$

20. $y - 4x$

21. $5.2x - y$

22. $xy - 10.1$

23. $14.3 - xy$

24. $3x - |y|$

LESSON 2.4

LESSON **2.4**	**Practice** *continued*
	For use with pages 73–79

25. Death Valley The lowest point in North America is at a place called Badwater in Death Valley, California. Its elevation is at -86 meters. What is this elevation in feet? *Hint:* Use the fact that 1 meter ≈ 3.281 feet.

26. Lava Flow A kind of lava, block lava, is moving away from the base of a volcano at a rate of 1.5 meters per day. If the lava continues to flow at this rate, how far away will the lava flow from the base of the volcano in 30 days?

27. Snow Melt After a recent snowfall, the snow on the ground in a shaded area is melting at a rate of 0.01 inch per minute. Currently, there are 4 inches of snow on the ground. If the snow continues melting at this rate, how much snow will be on the ground in 6 hours? How much snow will have melted?

28. City Population In 1990, the population of the Pittsburgh, Pennsylvania area was 1679 thousand people. The table shows the average rate of change in the population for two periods of time. Find the total population in 2000 and 2002.

Time period	Rate of change (thousand people/yr)
1990–2000	-3.7
2000–2002	-6.5

LESSON 2.5 **Practice**

For use with pages 81–86

CA Standards
Alg. 1.0
Alg. 1.1
Alg. 25.2

Use the distributive property to write an equivalent expression.

1. $5(x + 11)$

2. $3(x - 12)$

3. $-4(x + 8)$

4. $9(2x + 1)$

5. $(x - 7)(-10)$

6. $(4x + 3)5$

7. $x(4x - 1)$

8. $2x(x - 1)$

9. $-x(5x + 2)$

Identify the terms, like terms, coefficients, and constant terms of the expression.

10. $-8 + 2x + 5 + 11x$

11. $4x^2 + 1 - 3x^2 + 5$

12. $7y^2 - 6 + 3y^2 - 15$

13. $3xy + 5 - 2xy + 10$

Simplify the expression.

14. $6 + 10x + 3$

15. $2(3x + 1) + 4x$

16. $6(5 - x) + 12x$

17. $7(x - 1) - 5$

18. $8x + 3(2x - 1)$

19. $-2(x + 4) - 3$

20. $11x - (x + 7)$

21. $9 - 2(x - 4)$

22. $7x - 3(4 - 2x)$

LESSON 2.5

Name _____   Date _____

LESSON
2.5 **Practice** *continued*
For use with pages 81–86

23. Curtains You are making curtains by alternating strips of solid colored fabric and patterned fabric. The solid colored fabric costs $.99 per strip and the patterned fabric costs $1.25 per strip. You need 7 strips for one curtain. Write an equation that gives the total cost c in terms of the number n of solid colored strips used. Then find the total cost if you use 3 solid colored strips.

24. Shoe Boxes A department store is selling its plastic shoe boxes for $1.50 off the regular price of a shoe box. You buy 4 shoe boxes. Write an equation that gives the total cost t in terms of the regular cost r of a shoe box. Then find the total cost if the boxes regularly cost $3.59 each.

25. Delivering Papers You and your friend share a paper route. You can deliver 4 papers in one minute and your friend can deliver 3 papers in one minute. Seventy-five papers have to be delivered each day on the route. Let n be the number of papers you deliver.

   a. Use the verbal model to write an equation that you can use to find out how long it will take the two of you working together to deliver the papers.

| Total amount of time (min) | = | Your rate (min/paper) | · | Number of papers you deliver (papers) | + | Friend's rate (min/papers) | · | Number of papers friend delivers (papers) |

   b. How long will it take the two of you to deliver the papers if you deliver 38 papers? 50 papers?

Practice
For use with pages 88–93

CA Standards
Alg. 1.0
Alg. 1.1
Alg. 2.0

Find the multiplicative inverse of the number.

1. -7

2. $-\dfrac{1}{5}$

3. $-\dfrac{7}{8}$

Find the quotient.

4. $-32 \div (-2)$

5. $-1 \div \left(-\dfrac{6}{5}\right)$

6. $14 \div \left(-\dfrac{2}{7}\right)$

7. $17 \div \left(-2\dfrac{1}{8}\right)$

8. $-\dfrac{3}{4} \div 4$

9. $-\dfrac{1}{3} \div \dfrac{1}{5}$

10. $-\dfrac{1}{9} \div (-8)$

11. $-\dfrac{6}{11} \div (-3)$

12. $\dfrac{5}{8} \div \left(-2\dfrac{1}{2}\right)$

Find the mean of the numbers.

13. $1, -3, -10$

14. $-15, 4, -22$

15. $-7.5, 3, -6.5$

Simplify the expression.

16. $\dfrac{-8x + 27}{9}$

17. $\dfrac{15x - 5}{-5}$

18. $\dfrac{12x - 20}{-4}$

19. **Melting Point** The melting point of the element fluorine is $-219.62°C$. The melting point of the element bromine is $-7.2°C$. How many times lower is the melting point of fluorine than the melting point of bromine? Round your answer to the nearest tenth.

Practice *continued*
For use with pages 88–93

20. Website Traffic During a 3-month period, the traffic to a website dropped by 126,000 visitors. Find the average rate of change in the traffic to the website (in visitors per month) over the 3-month period.

21. Average Velocity The velocity of an object indicates the object's speed and the direction in which the object is traveling. A negative velocity indicates that the object is moving downward or backward. A hawk is diving downward at a rate of 50 feet in 28 seconds. Find the hawk's average velocity (in feet per second). Round your answer to the nearest tenth.

22. Health Club The table below shows change in the number of memberships at a health club. What is the average monthly change in the number of memberships?

Month	Nov.	Dec.	Jan.	Feb.	Mar.
Change in number of memberships	18	10	40	−25	−15

23. Bank Account Activity During a 14-day period, there is the following activity on your bank account. You deposit $100, withdraw $75, deposit $85, and withdraw $150. What is the rate of change (in dollars per day) in your bank account? Round your answer to the nearest cent.

LESSON 2.7 **Practice**
For use with pages 94–101

Evaluate the expression.

1. $\pm\sqrt{81}$

2. $\pm\sqrt{25}$

3. $-\sqrt{400}$

4. $\sqrt{625}$

5. $\sqrt{4900}$

6. $\pm\sqrt{169}$

Approximate the square root to the nearest integer.

7. $-\sqrt{29}$

8. $\sqrt{108}$

9. $-\sqrt{53}$

10. $\sqrt{138}$

11. $-\sqrt{55}$

12. $\sqrt{640}$

Tell whether each number in the list belongs to each of the following sets: real numbers, rational numbers, irrational numbers, integers, and whole numbers. Then order the numbers from least to greatest.

13. $-\sqrt{16}, 3.2, -\frac{3}{2}, \sqrt{9}$

14. $\sqrt{5}, -6, 2.5, -\frac{24}{5}$

Rewrite the conditional statement in if-then form. Then tell whether the statement is *true* or *false*. If it is false, give a counterexample.

15. All whole numbers are integers.

16. All integers are whole numbers.

Evaluate the expression for the given value of x.

17. $14 + \sqrt{x}$ when $x = 16$

18. $\sqrt{x} - 5.5$ when $x = 4$

LESSON 2.7

19. $-9 \cdot \sqrt{x}$ when $x = 25$

20. $2\sqrt{x} - 1$ when $x = 100$

21. Park A local park is in the shape of a square and covers an area of 3600 square feet. Find the side length of the park.

22. Wall Poster You are considering buying a square wall poster that has an area of 6.25 square feet. Find the side length of the wall poster.

23. Road Sign The U.S. Department of Transportation determines the sizes of the traffic control signs that you see along the roadways. The square Pennsylvania state route sign at the right has an area of 1296 square inches. Find the side length of the sign.

24. Flower Bed You are building the square flower bed shown using railroad ties. You want to place another railroad tie on the diagonal to form two triangular beds. Find the length of the diagonal by using the expression $\sqrt{2s^2}$ where s is the side length of the flower bed. Round your answer to the nearest tenth.

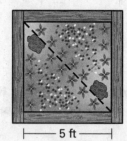

├── 5 ft ──┤

LESSON 2.8 Practice
For use with pages 102–108

CA Standards
Alg. 24.0
Alg. 25.0
Alg. 25.3

Determine whether inductive or deductive reasoning is used.

1. Derek solves ten problems involving subtraction of whole numbers. In each problem his answer is an even whole number. Derek concludes that the difference of any two whole numbers is an even whole number.

2. Luisa's answer to the addition problem $-3 + (-12) + (-17)$ is 32. Because she knows that the set of negative integers is closed under addition, Luisa concludes that her answer is incorrect.

3. Nel's baseball team is in first place, three games ahead of the second place team. Each team in the league has only two games left to play. So, Nel concludes that her team will end the regular season in first place.

4. Your uncle has visited you on New Year's Day in each of the past 3 years, so you conclude that he will visit you on New Year's Day again this year.

Tell which property of equality is illustrated by the statement.

5. If $r + s = t$ and $t = 16$, then $r + s = 16$.

6. If $x - 5 = 20$, then $x = 25$.

7. If $32°C = 0°F$, then $0°F = 32°C$.

LESSON 2.8

LESSON 2.8 Practice *continued*
For use with pages 102–108

In Exercises 8 and 9, perform the number trick for three different numbers and make a conjecture based on the results. Then prove the conjecture.

8. Choose any number. Triple the number. Then add 6. Then multiply by 4. Then divide by 6. Then subtract the original number.

9. Choose any number. Multiply twice the number by twice the number. Take the square root of the result. Then divide by 2.

10. Copy and complete the proof of this statement: $a \div (-a)$ is equal to -1.

$$a \div (-a) = a \times \left(-\frac{1}{a}\right) \qquad \underline{\qquad ? \qquad}$$
$$= -\left(a \times \frac{1}{a}\right) \qquad \text{Different signs; product is negative.}$$
$$= \underline{\quad ? \quad} \qquad \text{Inverse property of multiplication}$$

11. Copy and complete the proof of this statement: If $a = b$, then $a - c = b - c$.

$$a = b \qquad \text{Write original equation.}$$
$$a + (-c) = b + (-c) \qquad \underline{\qquad ? \qquad}$$
$$\underline{\qquad ? \qquad} \qquad \text{Subtraction rule for real numbers}$$

Name _____   Date _____

Solve the equation. Check your solution.

1. $x + 16 = 25$

2. $n - 9 = 17$

3. $-30 = w + 8$

4. $y + 5 = -13$

5. $a - 17 = -10$

6. $41 = 52 + m$

7. $c - 2.4 = 1.8$

8. $z + 4.1 = 9.6$

9. $-3.2 = 4.5 + p$

10. $9x = 54$

11. $-5b = 55$

12. $-42 = 3m$

13. $-52 = -4y$

14. $\frac{1}{3}n = 36$

15. $-\frac{3}{4}a = 12$

16. $0.5y = 17$

17. $-1.4a = 2.8$

18. $-6.5 = -1.3m$

Find the value of x for the rectangle or triangle.

19. Area = 70 in.^{2}

10 in.

20. Area = 30 in.^{2}

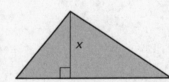

12 in.

LESSON 3.1

LESSON 3.1 **Practice** *continued*
For use with pages 125–131

21. **Caves** Cumberland Caverns in Tennessee is 44.4 kilometers long. This cave is 10.9 kilometers longer than Carlsbad Caverns in New Mexico. How long is Carlsbad Caverns?

22. **Bocce** Bocce is a lawn bowling game that originated in Italy. The bocce court below has an area of 1032 square feet. The width of the court is 12 feet. What is the length of the court?

12 ft

23. **Speedskating** In the 2006 Winter Olympics, Svetlana Zhurova won the 500-meter race. Her winning time was 76.57 seconds. Find her average speed to the nearest tenth of a meter per second.

24. **Part-Time Job** You work at a grocery store part-time. You estimate that you spend $\frac{3}{5}$ of your time stocking shelves. You stocked shelves for 18 hours this week. How many total hours did you work?

LESSON 3.1

LESSON 3.2 Practice
For use with pages 132–137

CA Standards
AF 4.1

Solve the equation. Check your solution.

1. $3n + 14 = 35$

2. $7y - 10 = 11$

3. $14 = 9 - x$

4. $9c - 5 = 13$

5. $4.6 = 4m - 3.4$

6. $1.2 = 2.4 - 3b$

7. $\dfrac{p}{6} + 9 = 14$

8. $\dfrac{w}{7} - 2 = 9$

9. $\dfrac{z}{3} - 8 = -4$

Write an equation for the verbal sentence. Then find the value of x.

10. The value of y is 5 more than 2 times the value of x. Find x when y is 17.

11. The value of y is 10 more than 4 times the value of x. Find x when y is -26.

12. The value of y is 14 less than 6 times the value of x. Find x when y is 22.

Solve the equation. Check your solution.

13. $9a + 4a = 26$

14. $14y - 6y = 48$

15. $38 = 26x - 7x$

16. $16x - 3x = -52$

17. $-9 = 11m - 8m$

18. $4.5z - 2.5z = 24$

LESSON 3.2

LESSON 3.2 | **Practice** *continued*
For use with pages 132–137

19. **Yoga Class** A fitness center offers yoga classes for $10 per class and sells yoga mats for $19.95. A person paid a total of $139.95 to the fitness center for yoga classes and a mat. Find the number of yoga classes the person took.

20. **Library Books** Your school has a $1200 grant to buy books and magazine subscriptions for the school library. The average cost of a magazine subscription is $30. Your school decides to spend $870 on books and the remaining amount on magazine subscriptions. How many magazine subscriptions can the school buy?

21. **Walking** You have already walked 5 miles of an 18-mile trail. If you walk the rest of the trail at a pace of 1 mile in 17 minutes, how many hours will it take you to finish the trail? Use the following verbal model to answer the question. Round your answer to the nearest tenth.

Walking rate (mi/min)	·	Number of minutes (min)	+	Number of miles already walked (mi)	=	Total number of miles walked (mi)

22. **Swimming Pool** The capacity of a small children's swimming pool is 106 gallons of water. There are currently 15 gallons of water in the pool. You are filling the pool with water at a rate of 2 gallons per minute.

   a. Write an equation that gives the amount y (in gallons) of water in the pool x minutes from now.

   b. After how many minutes will the pool be full?

LESSON 3.2

Name _____ Date _____

CA Standards
Alg 4.0

Solve the equation. Check your solution.

1. $16x - 15 - 9x = 13$

2. $15m + 4 - 9m = -32$

3. $3b - 9 - 8b = 11$

4. $-31 = 8 - 6p - 7p$

5. $9 + 4(x + 1) = 25$

6. $7(d - 5) + 12 = 5$

7. $10a + 5(a - 3) = 15$

8. $19a - 3(a - 6) = 66$

9. $\frac{1}{4}(x - 8) = 7$

10. $\frac{1}{3}(d + 9) = -12$

11. $\frac{3}{4}(n + 3) = 9$

12. $-\frac{5}{2}(w - 1) = 15$

13. $6.4 + 2.1(z - 2) = 8.5$

14. $4.5 - 1.5(6m + 2) = 6$

15. $15 = 4.3n - 2.1(n - 4)$

Find the value of x for the triangle or rectangle.

16. Perimeter = 23 feet

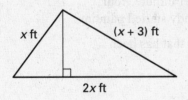

17. Perimeter = 24 meters

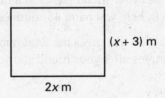

California Math, Algebra 1
Chapter 3 Practice Workbook

31

LESSON 3.3

LESSON 3.3 **Practice** *continued*
For use with pages 139–144

18. **Wrapping a Package** It takes 70 inches of ribbon to make a bow and wrap the ribbon around a box. The bow takes 32 inches of ribbon. The width of the box is 14 inches. What is the height of the box?

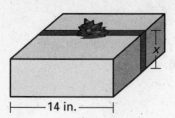

├── 14 in. ──┤

19. **Vacation** You are driving to a vacation spot that is 1500 miles away. Including rest stops, it takes you 42 hours to get to the vacation spot. You estimate that you drove at an average speed of 50 miles per hour. How many hours were you *not* driving?

20. **Moving** You helped a friend move a short distance recently. The friend rented a truck for $15 an hour and rented a dolly for $5. Your friend paid a total of $80 for the rental. For how long did your friend rent the truck?

21. **Painting** You and your friend are painting the walls in your apartment. You estimate that there is 1000 square feet of space to be painted. You paint at a rate of 4 square feet per minute and your friend paints at a rate of 3 square feet per minute. Your friend shows up to help you paint 45 minutes after you have already started painting.

a. Write an equation that gives the total number of square feet *y* that has been painted *x* minutes after your friend starts.

b. How long will it take you and your friend to finish painting? Round your answer to the nearest minute.

LESSON 3.3

LESSON 3.4 Practice

For use with pages 145–153

CA Standards
Alg 5.0

Solve the equation and describe each step you use.

1. $5x + 11 = 4x + 18$

2. $11p - 4 = 6p + 1$

3. $-6 = 2(w + 5)$

Solve the equation, if possible.

4. $15x - 8 = 14x + 13$

5. $9n - 7 = 5n + 5$

6. $4z - 15 = 4z + 11$

7. $-7a + 9 = 3a + 49$

8. $4(w + 3) = w - 15$

9. $8(y - 5) = 6y - 18$

10. $14m - 10 = 3(4 + m)$

11. $7 + x = \frac{1}{2}(4x - 2)$

12. $8b + 11 - 3b = 2b + 2$

13. $10d - 6 = 4d - 15 - 3d$

14. $16p - 4 = 4(2p - 3)$

15. $0.25(8z - 4) = z + 8 - 2z$

Find the perimeter of the square.

16.

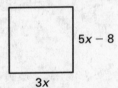

$5x - 8$

$3x$

17.

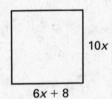

$10x$

$6x + 8$

18.

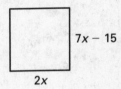

$7x - 15$

$2x$

19. Saving and Spending Currently, you have $80 and your sister has $145. You decide to save $6 of your allowance each week, while your sister decides to spend her whole allowance plus $7 each week. How long will it be before you have as much money as your sister?

LESSON 3.4 **Practice** *continued*
For use with pages 145–153

20. **Botanical Gardens** The membership fee for joining a gardening association is $24 per year. A local botanical garden charges members of the gardening association $3 for admission to the garden. Nonmembers of the association are charged $6. After how many visits to the garden is the total cost for members, including the membership fee, the same as the total cost for nonmembers?

21. **College Enrollment** Information about students' choices of majors at a small college is shown in the table. In how many years will there be 2 times as many students majoring in engineering than in business? In how many years will there be 2 times as many students majoring in engineering than in biology?

Major	Number of students enrolled in major	Average rate of change
Engineering	120	22 more students each year
Business	105	4 fewer students each year
Biology	95	6 more students each year

LESSON 3.5   **Practice**
For use with pages 155–160

Tell whether the ratio is in simplest form. If not, write it in simplest form.

1. 16 to 34

2. $17:65$

3. $\dfrac{33}{108}$

Solve the proportion. Check your solution.

4. $\dfrac{1}{2} = \dfrac{p}{14}$

5. $\dfrac{2}{3} = \dfrac{x}{21}$

6. $\dfrac{14}{8} = \dfrac{y}{20}$

7. $\dfrac{y}{6} = \dfrac{15}{9}$

8. $\dfrac{10}{15} = \dfrac{m}{39}$

9. $\dfrac{b}{8} = \dfrac{50}{20}$

10. $\dfrac{8}{2.5} = \dfrac{d}{0.5}$

11. $\dfrac{1.4}{1.6} = \dfrac{z}{10}$

12. $\dfrac{n}{4} = \dfrac{0.3}{1.5}$

Write the sentence as a proportion.

13. 5 is to 12 as x is to 48.

14. w is to 9 as 7 is to 36.

15. d is to 4 as 32 is to 56.

16. 22 is to 50 as x is to 500.

17. 10 is to 45 as b is to 225.

18. n is to 18 as 64 is to 72.

LESSON 3.5 **Practice** *continued*
For use with pages 155–160

19. **Books** Over the summer, you read 20 books. Eight of these books were biographies.

   a. Find the ratio of biographies to the total number of books.

   b. Find the ratio of non-biographies to biographies.

   c. Find the ratio of non-biographies to the total number of books.

20. **Fitness Center** The table shows the number of people attending classes at a fitness center during a recent evening.

Class	Aerobics	Spinning	Yoga
Number of people	32	28	16

   a. Find the ratio of the number of people taking yoga to the number of people taking spinning class.

   b. Find the ratio of the number of people taking aerobics to the total number of people taking classes.

21. **Mailroom** You work in the local mailroom at a college. One of your duties is to sort local mail from all of the other mail. You can sort 8 pieces of mail in 10 seconds. How many pieces of mail should you be able to sort in 45 minutes?

22. **Music** A music downloading website reports that nearly 5 out of every 7 songs downloaded are classified as pop music. According to this information, predict how many of the next 500 songs downloaded will be pop songs. Round your answer to the nearest whole number.

Practice
For use with pages 161–166

Name the cross products of the proportion.

1. $\dfrac{n}{11} = \dfrac{40}{55}$

2. $\dfrac{4}{9} = \dfrac{1}{x}$

3. $\dfrac{1.8}{1.9} = \dfrac{b}{3.8}$

4. $\dfrac{a+6}{21} = \dfrac{4}{7}$

5. $\dfrac{5x}{x+1} = \dfrac{30}{9}$

6. $\dfrac{2.2}{3.3} = \dfrac{a-2}{a-1}$

Solve the proportion.

7. $\dfrac{3}{5} = \dfrac{21}{m}$

8. $\dfrac{12}{7} = \dfrac{60}{d}$

9. $\dfrac{24}{x} = \dfrac{48}{60}$

10. $\dfrac{5}{7} = \dfrac{3w}{21}$

11. $\dfrac{2w}{16} = \dfrac{30}{80}$

12. $\dfrac{2z}{24} = \dfrac{6}{8}$

13. $\dfrac{8}{9} = \dfrac{30+a}{45}$

14. $\dfrac{9-y}{44} = \dfrac{5}{22}$

15. $\dfrac{26}{15} = \dfrac{104}{70-w}$

16. $\dfrac{35}{16} = \dfrac{c-8}{2}$

17. $\dfrac{1}{9} = \dfrac{a}{a+24}$

18. $\dfrac{2}{n} = \dfrac{14}{n+30}$

A map has a scale of 1 in. : 38 ft. Use the given map distance to find the actual distance.

19. 5.5 in.

20. 2.25 in.

21. 1.75 in.

Practice continued
For use with pages 161–166

22. **Concrete** You are making up your own mix of concrete to patch a set of stairs. In order to have the proper mix, you need to mix 1 part of Portland cement with 2 parts of sand and 3 parts of gravel.

   a. How many total parts are in one batch of concrete?

   b. You make a mix with 4 parts of sand. How many total parts of cement, sand, and gravel are in your mix?

23. **Architectural Firm** An architectural firm makes a model of a science center they are building. The ratio of the model to the actual size is 1 in.: 85 ft. Find the height of the building if the model is 1.5 inches tall.

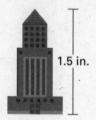

1.5 in.

24. **Tall Buildings** You made a model of the Space Needle in Seattle, Washington, for a report on architecture in the United States. You used a scale of 1 in.: 50 ft. Your model is 12.1 inches tall. Find the actual height of the Space Needle.

LESSON 3.6

LESSON 3.7

Practice

For use with pages 167–173

CA Standards
AF 3.1

Solve the literal equation for *x*. Then use the solution to solve the specific equation.

1. $ax + cx = b$; $3x + 5x = 8$

2. $a = \dfrac{c - x}{b}$; $6 = \dfrac{33 - x}{5}$

3. $\dfrac{a}{b} = \dfrac{c}{x}$; $\dfrac{9}{15} = \dfrac{12}{x}$

4. $cx - b = bx - a$; $7x - 3 = 3x - 11$

Solve the equation for *y*.

5. $4x + y = -10$

6. $6 - y = 17x$

7. $y - 3x - 11 = 0$

8. $2x + 2y = 8$

9. $6x - 3y = 12$

10. $16 - 8y = 4x$

11. $5x - 7y = 14$

12. $9y - 4x - 9 = 0$

13. $15 + 3y = -24x$

14. $4 + 6y = 12x - 2$

15. $4 - 10y = 22 - 6x$

16. $8x - 2y - 5 = 11$

Solve the formula for the indicated variable.

17. Area of a trapezoid: $A = \dfrac{h}{2}(b_1 + b_2)$. Solve for h.

18. Area of a rhombus: $A = \dfrac{1}{2}d_1d_2$. Solve for d_1.

LESSON 3.7

19. Guitar Practice You practice playing your guitar every day. You spend 15 minutes practicing chords and the rest of the time practicing a new song. So the total number of minutes y you practice for the week is given by $y = 7(15 + x)$, where x is the number of minutes you spend on practicing a new song.

a. Solve the equation for x.

b. How many minutes did you spend on a new song if you practiced 210 minutes last week? 245 minutes? 315 minutes?

20. Discounts Solve for r in the formula $S = L - rL$ where S is the sale price, L is the list price, and r is the discount rate.

a. An item with a list price of \$128 goes on sale for \$51.20. Find the discount rate.

b. An item with a list price of \$56.80 goes on sale for \$36.92. Find the discount rate.

21. Cookbook You bought a cookbook while on a recent trip overseas. All of the oven temperatures are in degrees Celsius and the only formula you can remember for temperature is how to convert Fahrenheit to Celsius: $C = \frac{5}{9}(F - 32)$.

a. Solve the equation for F.

b. A recipe tells you to bake a pie in the oven at 149°C. What is this temperature in degrees Fahrenheit? Round your answer to the nearest whole degree.

LESSON 4.1

Practice

For use with pages 189–194

CA Standards
Gr. 7 AF. 4.1

Write an inequality that is represented by the graph.

1.

2.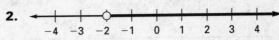

3.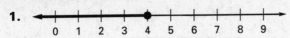

4.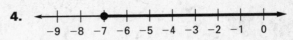

5.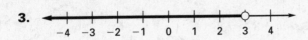

6.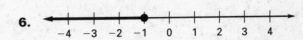

Solve the inequality. Graph your solution.

7. $x + 7 > 1$

8. $n - 3 \leq 9$

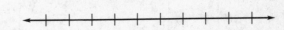

9. $10 \geq a + 7$

10. $m - 3 < -2$

11. $p - 5 > -5$

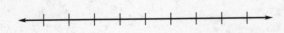

12. $x + 3 \leq -4.5$

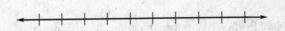

LESSON 4.1

Name _____   Date _____

13. $b + 9.5 \leq -6.4$

14. $y + 2.5 < 7.3$

15. $z - 10.2 > 18.3$

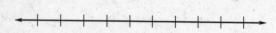

16. $d - 8 > 2.2$

Write the verbal sentence as an inequality. Then solve the inequality and graph your solution.

17. The sum of 15 and n is less than 8.

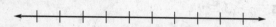

18. The difference of m and 3 is greater than or equal to 10.

19. Twenty-four is less than or equal to the sum of 35 and x.

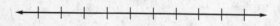

20. Eighty-five is greater than the difference of x and 63.

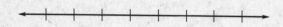

LESSON 4.1

Practice *continued*
For use with pages 189–194

21. Summer Reading During the summer you want to read at least 32 books. You have read 21 books so far this summer. What are the possible numbers of books you can read to pass your goal?

22. Baseball Hats You are a big baseball fan. You have a goal of attending a baseball game in every major league stadium in the country. Every time you go to a different stadium, you buy a baseball hat. You keep your hats in a display case that holds 25 hats. You have 8 baseball hats so far. What are the possible numbers of hats you can collect without needing another display case?

23. Gift Card You received a $25 gift card to a sporting goods store for your birthday. You are looking at skateboards and want to spend no more than $85 of your own money.

    a. Write and solve an inequality to find the prices p in dollars of skateboards you can buy.

    b. What is the most expensive skateboard you can buy?

24. Video Games You and your friend are having a video game competition. The person with the highest score after two games wins. The table shows your friend's first and second scores and your first score.

Game	Friend's score	Your score
1	6532	5034
2	4887	?

    a. Write and solve an inequality to find the scores s that you can earn in your second game in order to beat your friend.

    b. Will you win if you earn 6392 points? 6385 points? 6377 points? *Justify* your answers.

LESSON 4.1

LESSON
4.2 **Practice**
For use with pages 195–201

CA Standards
AF 4.1

Match the verbal sentence with the inequality. Then solve the inequality.

1. The product of 3 and x is less than or equal to 18.

A. $\dfrac{x}{18} \geq 3$

2. The product of 18 and x is greater than or equal to 3.

B. $18x \geq 3$

3. The quotient of x and 18 is greater than or equal to 3.

C. $3x \leq 18$

Solve the inequality. Graph your solution.

4. $3y \geq 4$

5. $\dfrac{x}{2} < 6$

6. $\dfrac{m}{5} > -5$

7. $\dfrac{c}{-10} \leq -2$

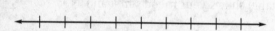

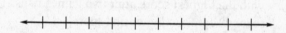

8. $8n > -1$

9. $42 < 6z$

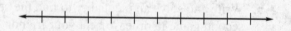

10. $-5p \leq 2$

11. $\dfrac{w}{-4} < 8$

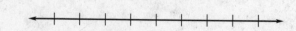

Name _____   Date _____

12. $-7a \geq -3$

13. $52 \leq -13x$

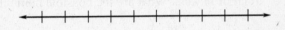

14. $0.25x > 18$

15. $-2d < 3$

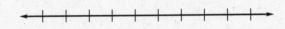

Write the verbal sentence as an inequality. Then solve the inequality and graph your solution.

16. The product of 12 and y is greater than or equal to 60.

17. The product of 7 and b is less than -35.

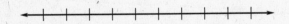

18. The quotient of m and 2 is greater than 23.

19. The quotient of p and 4.5 is less than or equal to 10.

LESSON 4.2

Practice *continued*
For use with pages 195–201

20. **Flower Beds** You are in charge of buying the flowers for the flower beds around your school. You cannot spend over $80 on flowers. The flowers cost $10.99 for a flat of flowers. What are the possible numbers of flats of flowers you can buy?

21. **Pavilion Rental** You and three of your friends decide to rent a pavilion at a local park for an end-of-the-school-year party. The group budget is $80. The group decides to split the cost equally.

   a. What are the possible amounts of money that each of you can spend?

   b. If two more of your friends decide to pitch in for the party, what are the possible amounts of money that each of you can spend if you all split the cost equally?

22. **Waiting Tables** Restaurants typically pay wait staff an hourly wage that is lower than minimum wage. The wait staff is expected to make up the difference in tips. The minimum wage is $5.15 per hour and a restaurant pays the wait staff $4 per hour.

   a. If a waitress works an 8-hour shift, write and solve an inequality that gives the total tips t in dollars that the waitress must earn in an 8-hour shift in order to meet or exceed the minimum wage.

   b. If the waitress makes $10.40 in tips during an 8-hour shift, will she meet or exceed the minimum wage? By how much?

   c. If the waitress makes $9.20 in tips during an 8-hour shift, will she meet or exceed the minimum wage? By how much?

LESSON 4.3 **Practice**
For use with pages 202–207

Solve the inequality. Graph your solution.

1. $4x - 7 \geq 1$

2. $7p + 3 < -11$

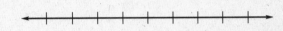

3. $8 - 2n \geq 26$

4. $3(a - 4) \leq 33$

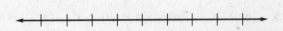

5. $6(y + 1) > 6$

6. $-2(c - 1) < -22$

7. $8m - 7 < 4m + 5$

8. $10 - 11d > -5d - 4$

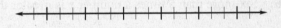

9. $9z \leq -7z + 14$

10. $6w + 3 < 2w + 15$

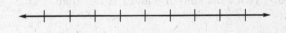

Solve the inequality, if possible.

11. $6y - 9 \leq 4y + 2y - 16$

12. $7p - 11p + 3 \geq 3 - 4p$

13. $4(c - 5) < 2(c - 10)$

14. $5(a - 3) \leq 5a - 6$

LESSON 4.3

15. $6(x - 8) > 6x - 48$

16. $2(3d - 4) < 4 + 6d - 15$

17. $4m + 14 - 2m \leq 2(m + 7)$

18. $-2(n - 3) \geq 1 - 2n + 5$

19. $4(3 - 2x) > 2(6 - 4x)$

20. $2(5 - a) > 4a + 13 - 6a$

21. $-4n + 11 < -4(n + 6)$

22. $3(5 - 6x) \leq 2(11 - 9x)$

23. $2m + 10 - 7m \leq 5(4 - m)$

24. $6(1 - 2n) \leq 5 - 12n$

Translate the verbal phrase into an inequality. Then solve the inequality and graph your solution.

25. Six more than 5 times a number x is greater than or equal to 31.

26. Twice the sum of 4 and x is less than -16.

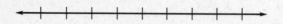

27. The difference of $10x$ and $3x$ is less than or equal to the sum of $4x$ and 21.

LESSON 4.3 **Practice** *continued*
For use with pages 202–207

28. The sum of $2x$ and $4x$ is greater than or equal to the sum of $3x$ and 36.

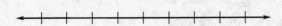

29. The difference of $2x$ and 15 is less than or equal to the sum of $4x$ and 17.

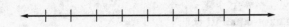

30. **Weaving** A weaver spends $420 on supplies to make wall hangings and plans to sell the wall hangings for $80 each.

   a. Write an inequality that gives the possible numbers w of wall hangings the weaver needs to sell in order for the profit to be positive.

   b. What are the possible numbers of wall hangings the weaver needs to sell in order for the profit to be positive?

31. **School Spirit** Your club is in charge of making pins that students can buy to show their school spirit for the upcoming football game. You have made 225 pins so far, and you only have 2 hours left to make the rest of the pins. You need to make at least 400 pins.

   a. Write an inequality that gives the possible numbers p of pins you have to make per minute in order to exceed your goal.

   b. What are the possible numbers of pins you have to make per minute in order to exceed your goal?

32. **Aquarium** You are getting a larger aquarium for your neon tetra fish and you also want to add more neon tetras to the larger aquarium. The general rule is that each fish needs 2 gallons of water. You currently have 6 neon tetras. If you buy a 20-gallon aquarium, what are the possible numbers of fish you can put in your aquarium? *Explain* how you got your answer.

LESSON 4.3

LESSON 4.4 Practice
For use with pages 209–218

CA Standards
Alg. 4.0
Alg. 5.0

Translate the verbal phrase into an inequality. Then graph the inequality.

1. All real numbers that are less than or equal to -3 *and* greater than or equal to -8

2. All real numbers that are greater than 5 *or* less than or equal to -1

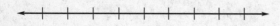

3. All real numbers that are greater than or equal to -2.5 *and* less than 3.5

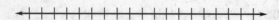

Solve the inequality. Graph your solution.

4. $-3 < x + 1 \leq 5$

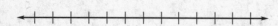

5. $-7 < x - 8 < 2$

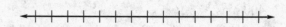

6. $-5 < -5x \leq 20$

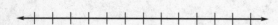

7. $0 \leq 2(x - 3) < 8$

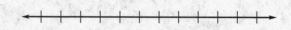

8. $3x + 2 < 8$ *or* $-x + 3 < -2$

9. $2(x + 4) < 6$ *or* $-x - 3 \leq -7$

LESSON
4.4 **Practice** *continued*
For use with pages 209–218

10. $5x < -30 \text{ or } x + 10 > 7$

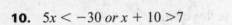

11. $3x + 5 \le 1 \text{ or } 8 - x < 5$

Write the verbal sentence as an inequality. Then solve the inequality and graph your solution.

12. Three times x is less than -6 *and* greater than -21.

13. One less than x is less than -1 *or* 3 more than x is greater than or equal to 7.

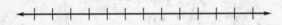

14. The difference of $2x$ and 5 is greater than -3 *and* less than or equal to 11.

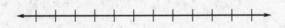

15. The sum of $3x$ and 1 is greater than -5 *and* less than or equal to 10.

16. **Temperature** The high temperature in a city last year was 95°F. The low temperature in this city last year was -5°F. Write and graph a compound inequality that represents the temperatures T throughout the year.

LESSON 4.4

LESSON 4.4 | **Practice** *continued*
For use with pages 209–218

17. Pollen Count Weather forecasts will often give reports on the pollen count. For people suffering from allergies, the pollen count indicates the severity of their symptoms. If a pollen count is high, the severity of the symptoms are increased. The table shows ranges for high, medium, and low pollen counts. Write an inequality to find the range at which the pollen count is not medium.

Pollen Count	High	Medium	Low
Range	Greater than 8	Greater than 4 and less than or equal to 8	Less than or equal to 4

18. Distances You live 5 miles from work and the gym you go to is 3 miles from work.

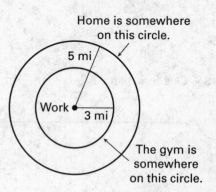

Home is somewhere on this circle.

The gym is somewhere on this circle.

a. Find the minimum distance *d* between your home and the gym.

b. Find the maximum distance *d* between your home and the gym.

c. Write an inequality that describes the possible distances *d* between your home and the gym.

Practice
For use with pages 220–225

Solve the equation.

1. $|x| = 9$

2. $|x| = 2.25$

3. $|x| = \dfrac{3}{2}$

4. $|x - 6| = 14$

5. $|x + 1| = 8$

6. $|2x - 3| = 15$

7. $|4x + 1| = 15$

8. $|7x + 2| = 23$

9. $|5 - 2x| = 9$

10. $3|2x - 2| = 18$

11. $4|5x - 1| = 36$

12. $2|6x + 5| - 1 = 25$

Solve the equation, if possible.

13. $|x + 3| - 4 = -1$

14. $|x - 8| - 9 = -5$

15. $|x + 3| + 2.5 = 3$

16. $-6|10 - 2x| = 24$

17. $-3|4x + 3| = -9$

18. $-4|5 + 2x| = -16$

19. $-\dfrac{1}{3}|1 - 8x| = 2$

20. $|3x - 8| + 0.25 = 0.75$

21. $|6x + 5| - 1.3 = -1.9$

Practice *continued*
For use with pages 220–225

Find the values of *x* that satisfy the definition of absolute value for the given value and the given absolute deviation.

22. Given value: 3; absolute deviation: 5

23. Given value: 1; absolute deviation: 7

24. Given value: −4; absolute deviation: 2

25. Given value: −2.5; absolute deviation: 8

26. Food Scale Bakers will typically weigh out flour for recipes rather than use a measuring cup because weighing is a more accurate measure. A baker is using a scale that has an absolute error of 0.05 gram.

a. Find the minimum and maximum possible weights if the scale is used to measure out 225 grams of flour.

b. Find the minimum and maximum possible weights if the scale is used to measure out 300 grams of flour.

c. Find the minimum and maximum possible weights if the scale is used to measure out 420 grams of flour.

27. Toothpaste Prices The average price of the brand of toothpaste that you buy is $2.49 for an 8.2-ounce tube. Depending on where you shop, the prices vary by as much as $.15.

a. Write an absolute value equation that represents the minimum and maximum prices of the toothpaste.

b. Find the minimum and maximum prices of the toothpaste.

c. You have a coupon for $.50 off two tubes of toothpaste. If you go to the store that has the minimum price for the toothpaste, how much will you pay for two tubes?

Name _____ Date _____

Practice
For use with pages 226–231

Solve the inequality. Graph your solution.

1. $|x| \geq 5$

2. $|x| < 6.5$

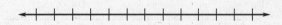

3. $|x| \geq \frac{3}{2}$

4. $|x - 6| \leq 1$

5. $|x + 7| > 11$

6. $|-x - 5| < 1$

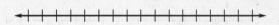

7. $|2x + 1| \geq 5$

8. $|3x - 2| \leq 7$

9. $|8 - 3x| \geq 7$

10. $\left|\frac{1}{2}x - 4\right| > 20$

11. $\left|1 - \frac{4}{3}x\right| < 5$

12. $2 - |x - 4| < -6$

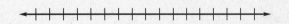

California Math, Algebra 1
Chapter 4 Practice Workbook **55**

Practice *continued*
For use with pages 226–231

Write the verbal sentence as an inequality. Then solve the inequality and graph your solution.

13. The distance between x and 8 is less than 14.

14. The distance between x and -5 is greater than or equal to 12.

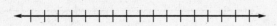

15. The distance between 9 and x is less than or equal to 8.

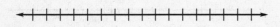

16. The distance between 10 and $2x$ is greater than 34.

Tell whether the statement is *true* or *false*. If it is false, give a counterexample.

17. If a is a solution of $|x + 4| < 7$, then a is also a solution of $x + 4 < 7$.

18. If a is a solution of $|x - 6| \geq 4$, then a is also a solution of $x - 6 \leq -4$.

19. **DVDs** The average price of a standard DVD is $15.99 with a standard deviation of $4. Write an absolute value inequality that describes this range in prices.

LESSON 4.6

Practice *continued*
For use with pages 226–231

20. Body Temperature A canine's body temperature is considered to be normal if it is 101°F with an absolute deviation of 1.5°F.

a. Write an absolute value inequality that represents the normal temperature range.

b. Solve the inequality. What is the normal temperature range?

21. Baseball A baseball should weigh 5.12 ounces with an absolute deviation of 0.035 ounce. The circumference of a baseball should be 9.05 inches with an absolute deviation of 0.05 inch.

a. Write absolute value inequalities that represent the ranges for the weight and circumference of a baseball.

b. Is a ball that weighs 5.16 ounces and has a circumference of 9 inches within the ranges that it should be? *Explain* why or why not.

c. What are the maximum and minimum circumferences of a baseball?

d. What are the maximum and minimum weights of a baseball?

LESSON 4.6

CA Standards
Alg. 16.0
Alg. 17.0
Alg. 18.0

LESSON 5.1 **Practice**
For use with pages 249–255

Complete the sentence.

1. The input variable is called the ___?___ variable.

2. The output variable is called the ___?___ variable.

Tell whether the pairing is a function.

3. $\{(1, 3), (2, 0), (4, 4)\}$ **4.** $\{(-1, 1), (7, 2), (8, 5)\}$ **5.** $\{(0, -5), (2, -1), (9, 7)\}$

Determine whether the relation is a function.

6.

x	2	3	4	5
y	4	7	10	13

7.

x	3	4	3	2
y	-2	3	2	4

Make a table for the function. Identify the range of the function.

8. $y = 4x - 2$ **9.** $y = 0.1x + 3$ **10.** $y = \frac{1}{2}x + 2$

Domain: 1, 2, 3, 4   Domain: 10, 20, 30, 40   Domain: 6, 7, 8, 9

Write a rule for the function.

11.

Input, x	1	2	3	4
Output, y	5	10	15	20

12.

Input, x	10	11	12	13
Output, y	3	4	5	6

LESSON 5.1 **Practice** *continued*
For use with pages 249–255

13. **Shoe Sizes** The table shows men's shoe sizes in the United States and Australia. Write a rule for the Australian size as a function of the United States' size.

U.S. size	5	6	7	8	9	10
Australian size	3	4	5	6	7	8

14. **Balloon Bunches** You are making balloon bunches to attach to tables for a charity event. You plan on using 8 balloons in each bunch. Write a rule for the total number of balloons used as a function of the number of bunches created. Identify the independent and dependent variables. How many balloons will you use if you make 10 bunches?

15. **Baking** A baker has baked 10 loaves of bread so far today and plans on baking 3 loaves more each hour for the rest of his shift. Write a rule for the total number of loaves baked as a function of the number of hours left in the baker's shift. Identify the independent and dependent variables. How many loaves will the baker make if he has 4 hours left in his shift?

LESSON 5.1

CA Standards
Alg. 17.0
Alg. 18.0

LESSON 5.2 **Practice B**
For use with pages 256–263

Graph the ordered pairs. Determine whether the graph represents a function.

1. (3, 4), (4, 7), (5, 10), (6, 13), (7, 16)

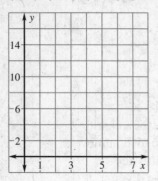

2. (2, 5), (6, 7), (4, 6), (12, 10), (10, 9)

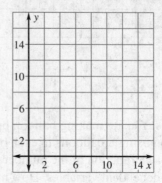

Complete the input-output table for the function.

3. $y = 3x + 2$

x	0	1	2	3
y				

4. $y = 4x - 1$

x	1	2	3	4
y				

Graph the function.

5. $y = 6 - x$

Domain: 6, 5, 4, 3, 2

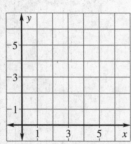

6. $y = \frac{1}{3}x$

Domain: 6, 9, 12, 15, 18

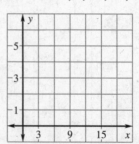

LESSON 5.2

**LESSON
5.2**
Practice B *continued*
For use with pages 256–263

CA Standards
Alg. 17.0
Alg. 18.0

7. $y = 4x - 3$

Domain: $-2, -1, 0, 1, 2$

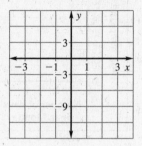

8. $y = 1.2x$

Domain: $1, 2, 3, 4, 5$

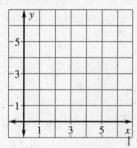

**Write a rule for the function represented by the graph. Identify the domain
and range of the function.**

9.

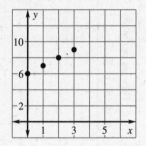

10.

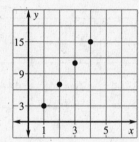

11.

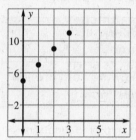

12.

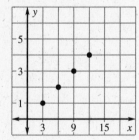

13.

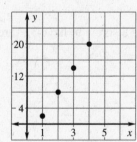

14.

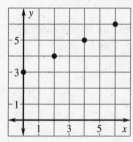

LESSON 5.2

LESSON 5.2

Practice B *continued*
For use with pages 256–263

15. **High Temperatures** The table shows the high temperature
    H (in degrees Fahrenheit) in a city during the week as a
    function of the number of days d since Monday. Graph the
    function. Describe how the high temperatures change as the
    week progresses.

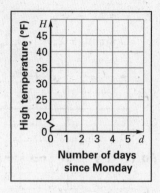

**Number of days
since Monday**

Number of days since Monday, *d*	0	1	2	3	4	5
High temperature (degrees Fahrenheit), *H*	24	34	41	39	37	39

16. **Metal Screws** The table shows the number of threads per inch on
    a screw as a function of screw size.

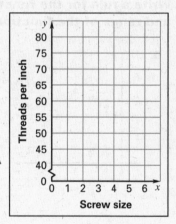

Screw size number, *x*	0	1	2	3	4	5	6
Number of threads per inch, *y*	80	72	64	56	48	44	40

a. Graph the function.

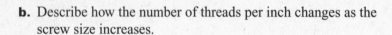

b. Describe how the number of threads per inch changes as the
   screw size increases.

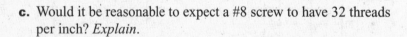

c. Would it be reasonable to expect a #8 screw to have 32 threads
   per inch? *Explain.*

LESSON 5.2

LESSON 5.3 **Practice**
For use with pages 264–272

CA Standards
Alg. 6.0
Alg. 7.0

Decide which of the two points lies on the graph of the line.

1. $2x + y = 10$

   a. $(4, 3)$ **b.** $(-4, 18)$

2. $x - 3y = 12$

   a. $(9, 1)$ **b.** $(6, -2)$

3. $2y - x = 9$

   a. $(5, 1)$ **b.** $(1, 5)$

Solve the equation for _y_.

4. $-6x + y = 11$

5. $8x + 2y = 10$

6. $6x - 3y = -9$

7. $-4x + 2y = 16$

8. $10x - 5y = 25$

9. $3x + 2y = -8$

Graph the equation.

10. $y + x = 14$

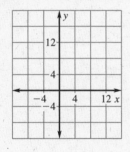

11. $y - 5x = 2$

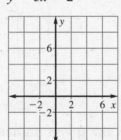

12. $2y - 4x = 10$

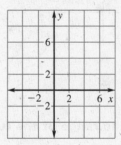

13. $x = -6$

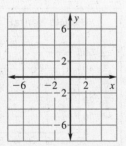

14. $y = 4$

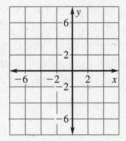

15. $3x - 2y = 0$

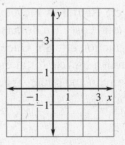

**LESSON
5.3** **Practice** *continued*
For use with pages 264–272

Graph the function with the given domain. Then identify the range of the function.

16. $y = 2x - 2$; domain: $x \geq 0$

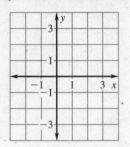

17. $y = -3x + 1$; domain: $x \leq 0$

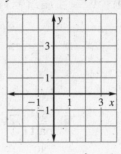

18. $y = 3$; domain: $x \leq 2$

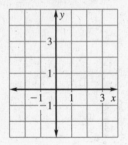

19. $y = -1$; domain: $x \geq -1$

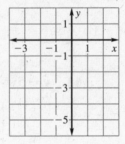

Identify the range of the function with the given domain.

20. $x + 3y = -8$; domain $x \geq 0$

21. $6x - 3y = 9$; domain: $x \leq 1$

22. **Bicycle Rental** A bicycle rental shop rents bicycles for $8 per hour. The total cost c (in dollars) for renting a bicycle h hours is given by the function $c = 8h$. Once you get to the rental shop, you figure you can rent a bicycle for at most 5 hours. Graph the function and identify its domain and range. What is the most that you will pay for renting the bicycle?

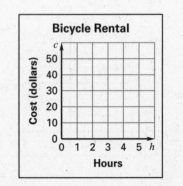

Bicycle Rental

California Math, Algebra 1

LESSON 5.5 **Practice** *continued*
For use with pages 281–289

28. $(x, -7), (1, 2); m = 3$ **29.** $(9, y), (3, 2); m = \frac{2}{3}$ **30.** $(7, 5), (x, 2); m = \frac{3}{4}$

31. Trolley Bus The table shows the number of trolley buses in operation in the United States during certain years.

Year	1980	1985	1990	1995	2000
Number of buses	823	676	832	885	951

a. *Describe* the rates of change in the number of buses during the time period.

b. Determine the time intervals during which the number of trolley buses showed the greatest and least rates of change.

32. Postage Rate The graph shows the cost (in dollars) to mail a letter that weighs one ounce during certain years.

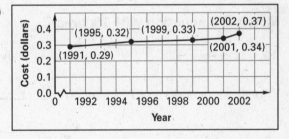

a. Determine the time interval during which the cost to mail a one-ounce letter showed the greatest rate of change.

b. Determine the time interval during which the cost to mail a one-ounce letter showed the least rate of change.

33. Heart Rate The graph shows the heart rate of a person during 30 minutes of exercise. Give a verbal description of the workout.

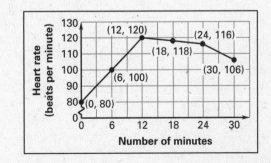

LESSON 5.6 Practice
For use with pages 290–296

Identify the slope and *y*-intercept of the line with the given equation.

1. $y = 5x - 4$

2. $y = 10 - 4x$

3. $9x + y = 8$

4. $12x + 3y = 9$

5. $6x - 2y = 2$

6. $2x + 5y = 10$

7. $9x - 3y = -1$

8. $4y + 6x = 2$

9. $8y - 2x = 5$

10. $5x + 5y = 3$

11. $-4y = 16$

12. $6x = 12$

Match the equation with its graph.

13. $3x + 4y = 12$

14. $3x + 4y = -12$

15. $3x - 4y = 12$

A.
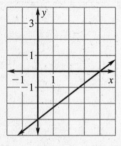

B.
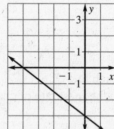

C.
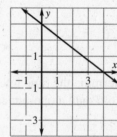

LESSON 5.6

Name _____ Date _____

Practice *continued*
For use with pages 290–296

Graph the equation.

16. $y = -7x + 2$

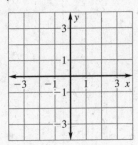

17. $y = 5x + 4$

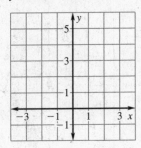

18. $y = -x + 9$

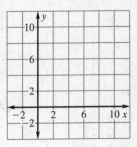

19. $y = \frac{1}{5}x$

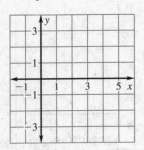

20. $y = -\frac{2}{3}x + 1$

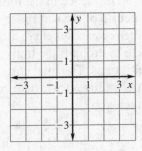

21. $y = \frac{4}{3}x - 5$

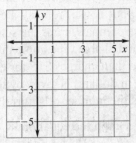

Determine which lines are parallel.

22.

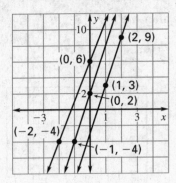

23.

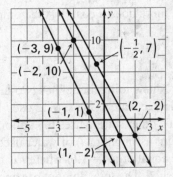

LESSON 5.6

Name _____ Date _____

Tell whether the graphs of the two equations are parallel lines.

24. $y = 8x - 3, 8x + y = 3$

25. $2x + y = 5, -6 + 2x = y$

26. $2x + y = 5, y = 0.5x - 3$

27. $y = -0.6x + 2, 5y + 3x = 8$

28. $8x + 3y = 9, 3y - 4 = 8x$

29. $10x + 2y = 7, 5x - y = 6$

30. Squirrels A family of squirrels takes up residence in the roof of your house. You call a company to get rid of the squirrels. The company traps the squirrels and then releases them in a wooded area. The company charges $30 to drop off the traps and then charges $15 for each squirrel it traps. The total cost C (in dollars) is given by the equation $C = 30 + 15s$ where s is the number of squirrels that are taken away.

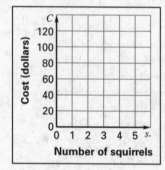

Number of squirrels

a. Graph the equation.

b. Suppose the company raises its fee to $18 to take away each squirrel so that the total cost for s squirrels is given by the equation $C = 30 + 18s$. Graph the equation in the same coordinate plane as the equation in part (a).

c. How much more does it cost for the company to trap 4 squirrels after the fee is raised?

31. Water Usage A new toilet model has two different flush settings in order to conserve water. One setting uses 1.6 gallons of water per flush and the other setting uses 0.8 gallon of water per flush. The total amount w (in gallons) of water used in the first setting is given by the equation $w = 1.6f$ where f is the number of times the toilet is flushed. The total amount of water used in the second setting is given by the equation $w = 0.8f$.

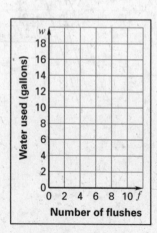

Number of flushes

a. Graph both equations in the same coordinate plane. What do the slopes and the w-intercepts mean in this situation?

b. How much more water is used by the first setting if the toilet is flushed 10 times?

Name _____   Date _____

Tell whether the equation represents direct variation. If so, identify the constant of variation.

1. $y = 8x$

2. $y = 2x + 1$

3. $3x + y = 6$

Graph the direct variation equation.

4. $y = 9x$

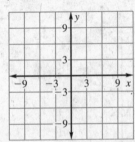

5. $y = -7x$

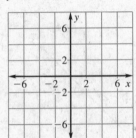

6. $3y = 4x$

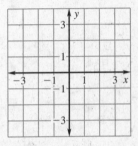

7. $4y = -12x$

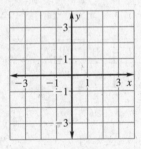

8. $8y = x$

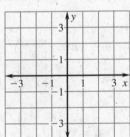

9. $8y = 6x$

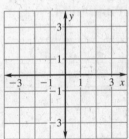

The graph of a direct variation equation is shown. Write the direct variation equation. Then find the value of *y* when *x* = 10.

10.

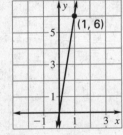
(1, 6)

11.

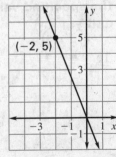
(−2, 5)

12.

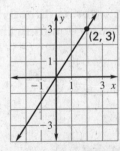
(2, 3)

LESSON 5.7

LESSON
5.7 **Practice** *continued*
For use with pages 297–303

13.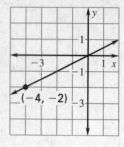

14.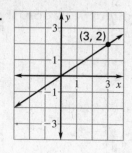

15.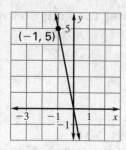

16.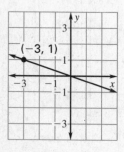

17.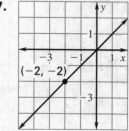

18.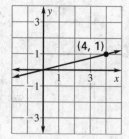

Tell whether the table represents direct variation. If so, write the direct variation equation.

19.

x	0.5	3	−2	1	−8
y	9	54	−36	18	−144

20.

x	−5	3	−2	10	20
y	−2	1.2	−0.8	4	8

21.

x	8	2	−4	−0.5	14
y	7	28	7	−112	4

22.

x	−0.2	−2	1	12	18
y	30	3	−6	−0.5	3

Given that y varies directly with x, use the specified values to write a direct variation equation that relates x and y.

23. $x = 24, y = 3$

24. $x = -16, y = -4$

25. $x = 28, y = -4$

Practice continued
For use with pages 297–303

26. $x = 5, y = -30$ **27.** $x = \dfrac{1}{6}, y = 1$ **28.** $x = 8, y = -3$

29. $x = 6, y = 102$ **30.** $x = -8, y = 64$ **31.** $x = 15, y = 9$

32. Hooke's Law The force F required to stretch a spring varies directly with the amount the spring is stretched s. Eight pounds is needed to stretch a spring 8 inches.

     a. Write a direct variation equation that relates F and s.

     b. How much force is required to stretch a spring 25 inches?

33. Basement Waterproofing One way to keep moisture out of your basement is to paint the walls with a waterproof paint. The amount of paint g (in gallons) you need varies directly with the area A of the basement. One gallon of paint covers 100 square feet.

     a. Write a direct variation equation that relates g and A.

     b. How many gallons do you need to cover 530 square feet?

     c. How many square feet does 8.5 gallons of paint cover?

34. Downloading Files The table shows the amount of time t (in seconds) it takes to download a file of size s (in kilobytes).

     a. *Explain* why s varies directly with t.

     b. Write a direct variation equation that relates s and t.

     c. How long will it take to download an 800-kilobyte file? Round your answer to the nearest second.

Time, t (sec)	File size, s (kb)
15	420
30	840
45	1260

LESSON 6.1 Practice
For use with pages 321–328

CA Standards
Alg. 7.0

Write an equation of the line with the given slope and y-intercept.

1. slope: 7; y-intercept: 4   **2.** slope: -3; y-intercept: 5   **3.** slope: 1; y-intercept: -6

Write an equation of the line shown.

4.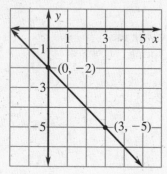

5.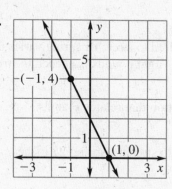

6.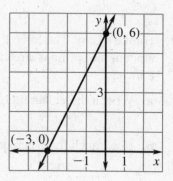

Write an equation of the line that passes through the given points.

7. $(-1, 0), (0, -2)$ **8.** $(0, 4), (6, 13)$ **9.** $(4, 5), (8, 2)$

10. $(-1, -9), (6, 5)$ **11.** $(2, -13), (-3, 12)$ **12.** $(-4, -21), (1, -1)$

Find the value of m or b if the given line passes through the given point.

13. $y = mx + 2; (3, -7)$ **14.** $y = 5x + b; (5, 15)$

15. **Landscape Supply** A landscape supply business charges $30 to deliver mulch. The mulch costs $23 per cubic yard.

a. Write an equation that gives the total cost (in dollars) of having mulch delivered to a site as a function of the number of cubic yards ordered.

b. Find the cost of having 8 cubic yards of mulch delivered to a site.

California Math, Algebra 1

| LESSON 6.1 | **Practice**
continued

16. **Cable Television** A cable company charges $44 per month for basic service. Each premium channel costs an additional $16 per month.

    a. Write an equation that gives the total cost (in dollars) of cable each month as a function of the number of premium channels.

    b. Find the number of premium channels you can have for $80 a month.

17. **Laser Printer** A laser printer has a "sleep" mode that is an energy-saving feature. When a job is sent to the printer, it takes 45 seconds for the printer to warm up and then the printer prints pages at a rate of 6 pages per minute.

    a. Write the time it takes the printer to warm up in minutes.

    b. Write an equation that gives the total amount of time (in minutes) it takes the printer to warm up and print a job as a function of the number of pages in the job.

    c. Find out how long it takes the printer to print a 50-page job if it must first warm up.

Name _____ Date _____

Write an equation of the line that passes through the given point and has slope *m*.

1. $(-1, 6); m = 5$

2. $(10, 3); m = -2$

3. $(2, -3); m = 7$

4. $(-4, -9); m = 2$

5. $(5, -4); m = \dfrac{1}{3}$

6. $(-8, 1); m = -\dfrac{3}{4}$

Write an equation of the line shown.

7.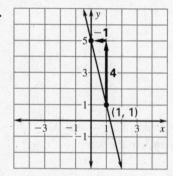

8.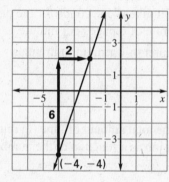

9.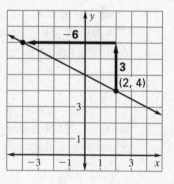

Write an equation of the line that passes through the given points.

10. $(-10, 7), (5, -3)$

11. $(-5, -3), (12, 17.4)$

12. $(-8, 84), (5, -46)$

13. **Oil Changes** You are scheduled to start your job at an oil change shop 2 hours after the shop opens. Two hours after you start, a total of 11 cars have had their oil changed since the shop opened. Three hours later, a total of 14 cars have had their oil changed. At what rate are cars getting their oil changed since you started working? How many cars had their oil changed before you started work?

LESSON 6.2 **Practice** *continued*
For use with pages 329–336

14. **Motor Vehicle Licenses** The amount of revenue brought in by states from motor vehicle licenses increased at a relatively constant rate of 499.79 million dollars per year from 1990 to 2000. In 2000, the states brought in 15,099 million dollars in revenue from motor vehicle licenses.

   a. What was the approximate revenue (in million dollars) from licenses in 1990?

   b. Write an equation that gives the revenue (in million dollars) as a function of the number of years since 1990.

   c. Find the revenue from licenses in 1999.

15. **Imports** The number of metric tons of fruits, nuts, and vegetables imported into the United States increased at a relatively constant rate of 437.5 thousand metric tons per year from 1990 to 2002. In 2002, about 9900.5 thousand metric tons of fruits, nuts, and vegetables were imported. Write an equation that gives the number of thousand metric tons imported as a function of the number of years since 1990. Find the year in which the number of metric tons reached 8000 thousand metric tons.

Name _____ Date _____

Write an equation in point-slope form of the line that passes through the given point and has the given slope *m*.

1. $(1, 9)$; $m = -3$ **2.** $(4, -10)$; $m = 2$ **3.** $(-5, 6)$; $m = 4$

4. $(-2, -8)$; $m = 3$ **5.** $(-4, -7)$; $m = -\frac{1}{2}$ **6.** $(-9, 2)$; $m = -5$

7. $(6, -4)$; $m = \frac{2}{3}$ **8.** $(0, 15)$; $m = \frac{4}{5}$ **9.** $(-8, 0)$; $m = 2$

Graph the equation.

10. $y - 6 = 3(x - 4)$ **11.** $y + 1 = 2(x - 5)$ **12.** $y - 2 = -4(x + 3)$

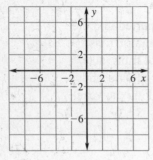 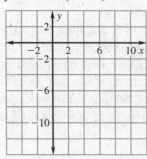 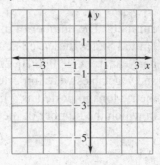

13. $y + 2 = -(x - 1)$ **14.** $y = \frac{1}{2}(x - 5)$ **15.** $y + 3 = 5x$

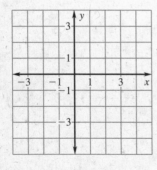 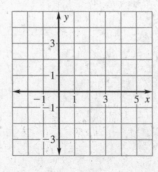 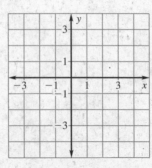

California Math, Algebra 1
Chapter 6 Practice Workbook

LESSON 6.3

Name _____   Date _____

Practice *continued*
For use with pages 340–346

16. $y + 1 = \frac{2}{3}(x + 1)$

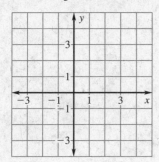

17. $y - 2 = -\frac{1}{2}(x - 3)$

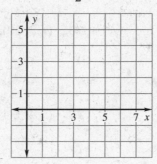

18. $y + \frac{1}{2} = 2(x - 1)$

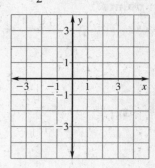

Write an equation in point-slope form of the line shown.

19.

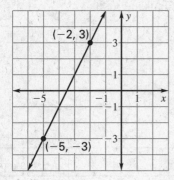

20.

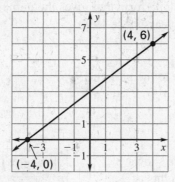

21.

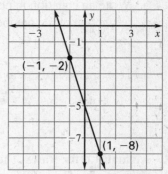

22.

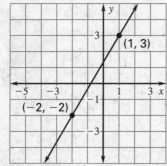

23.

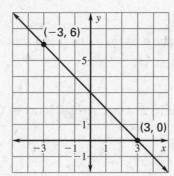

24.

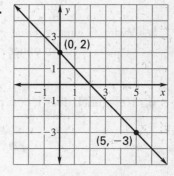

LESSON 6.3

California Math, Algebra 1
Chapter 6 Practice Workbook   **83**

LESSON 6.3 | **Practice** *continued*
For use with pages 340–346

Write an equation in point-slope form of the line that passes through the given points.

25. $(9, 4), (17, 6)$

26. $(-3, 10), (4, 2)$

27. $(3, -8), (7, -2)$

28. $(-4, -4), (2, 5)$

29. Bryce Canyon National Park From 1990 to 2000, the number of thousand visits by people to Bryce Canyon National Park increased by about 23.9 thousand visits per year. In 2000, there were about 1102.4 thousand visits to the park.

   a. Write an equation in point-slope form that gives the number of thousand visits as a function of the number of years since 1990.

   b. How many visits were made to the park in 1995?

30. Airmail Letter Rates The table shows the cost of mailing different weights of airmail letters to Canada in 2005.

Weight (oz)	2	3	4	8
Cost (dollars)	0.85	1.10	1.35	2.35

   a. *Explain* why the situation can be modeled using a linear equation.

   b. Write an equation that gives the cost (in dollars) as a function of the weight of an airmail letter (in ounces).

   c. How much does it cost to mail a 5-ounce airmail letter to Canada?

31. New Mexico The population density of New Mexico increased at a relatively constant rate from 1980 to 1999. In 1985, the population density was about 11.62 people per square mile. In 1999, the population density was about 14.28 people per square mile. Write an equation that gives the population density (in people per square mile) as a function of the number of years since 1980. What was the population density in 1990?

LESSON 6.3

LESSON 6.4 **Practice**
For use with pages 347–352

Write two equations in standard form that are equivalent to the given equation.

1. $6x + 24y = 18$

2. $8x - 14y = 2$

3. $6x + y = 1$

4. $-4x - 2y = 16$

5. $2x + 3y = 11$

6. $-9x + 4y = 5$

Write an equation in standard form of the line that passes through the given point and has the given slope *m*.

7. $(4, 3), m = 7$

8. $(5, -1), m = 2$

9. $(-2, 6), m = 1$

10. $(-7, 8), m = -3$

11. $(9, -10), m = -4$

12. $(-15, -4), m = \frac{1}{2}$

Write an equation in standard form of the line that passes through the two given points.

13. $(2, 6), (3, 8)$

14. $(-1, 2), (5, 4)$

15. $(7, -3), (4, 1)$

16. $(3, -8), (5, -9)$

17. $(-5, 6), (2, -3)$

18. $(-3, -1), (6, -8)$

Write equations of the horizontal and the vertical lines that pass through the given point.

19. $(8, 3)$

20. $(-2, 6)$

21. $(5, -5)$

LESSON 6.4 Practice *continued*
For use with pages 347–352

22. Text Messaging Your cell phone plan charges you $.02 to send a text message and $.07 to receive a text message. You plan to spend no more than $5 a month on text messaging.

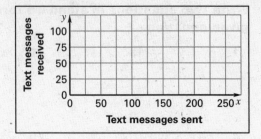

a. Write an equation in standard form that models the possible combinations of sent text messages and received text messages.

b. Graph the equation from part (a). *Explain* what the intercepts of the graph mean in this situation.

c. List three other possible combinations of the number of messages you can send and receive.

23. Potting Soil Mix You are making 24 pounds of your own potting soil mix of sphagnum peat moss and coarse sand. You buy the peat moss in bags that weigh approximately 2 pounds.

a. The last time you made potting soil, you used 9 bags of sphagnum peat moss and 4 bags of coarse sand. Use this information to find the number of pounds in a bag of coarse sand.

b. Write an equation in standard form that models the possible combinations of bags of sphagnum peat moss and coarse sand you can use.

c. List three possible combinations of whole bags of sphagnum peat moss and coarse sand you can use to make the potting soil.

LESSON 6.5 **Practice**
For use with pages 353–360

CA Standards
Alg. 8.0

Write an equation of the line that passes through the given point and is parallel to the given line.

1. $(4, 7)$, $y = 5x - 3$

2. $(3, -2)$, $y = \frac{2}{3}x + 1$

3. $(-6, 1)$, $4x + y = 7$

4. $(-5, -5)$, $6x - y = 1$

5. $(0, -8)$, $8x + 4y = 5$

6. $(-9, 11)$, $5x - 10y = 3$

Write an equation of the line that passes through the given point and is perpendicular to the given line.

7. $(1, -1)$, $y = 3x + 2$

8. $(5, 0)$, $y = \frac{2}{3}x - 4$

9. $(3, -7)$, $y = -\frac{1}{5}x + 1$

10. $(-9, 2)$, $10x - 5y = 6$

11. $(10, -11)$, $-2x + 5y = 1$

12. $(-4, -8)$, $8x + 3y = 7$

Determine which of the following lines, if any, are parallel or perpendicular.

13. Line a: $y = 8x - 5$, Line b: $y = \frac{1}{8}x + 1$, Line c: $8x + y = 2$

14. Line a: $y = -2x + 5$, Line b: $2y - x = 3$, Line c: $2x + y = 1$

15. Line a: $6x + 2y = 5$, Line b: $y = \frac{1}{3}x - 4$, Line c: $y = -3x + 5$

LESSON 6.5

Name _____   Date _____

16. Kite Design You are beginning to model a kite design on the coordinate plane, as shown.

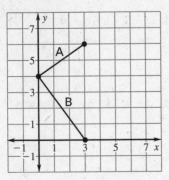

a. Write an equation that models part A of the kite.

b. Write an equation that models part B of the kite.

c. Do the kite parts form a right angle? *Justify* your answer.

17. Lunch Duty Everyone at camp takes turns being on lunch duty. Jamie and Kathleen are in charge of making sandwiches. They each can make 1 sandwich every 2 minutes. Jamie makes 5 sandwiches by the time Kathleen starts working at noon.

a. Write equations that model the number of sandwiches made by each person as a function of the number of minutes since noon.

b. How many sandwiches will each person make by 12:20 P.M.?

c. How are the graphs of the equations from part (a) related? Justify your answer.

Name _____   Date _____

Practice

For use with pages 375–382

Tell whether the ordered pair is a solution of the linear system.

1. $(4, 1)$;
$x + 2y = 6$
$3x + y = 11$

2. $(-2, 1)$;
$5x - 2y = -12$
$x + 3y = 1$

3. $(4, -3)$;
$-3x + 2y = -18$
$6x - y = 27$

4. $(-4, -6)$;
$3x - y = 6$
$-x + 2y = 8$

5. $(-4, 3)$;
$4x + 3y = -12$
$x + 2y = -6$

6. $(-2, -5)$;
$-x + y = -3$
$-x + 3y = -13$

Use the graph to solve the linear system. Check your solution.

7. $x - y = 8$
$x + y = -2$

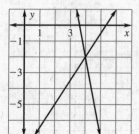

8. $5x - y = -9$
$y + 2x = 2$

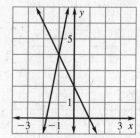

9. $2x + 3y = 2$
$-2x + y = 6$

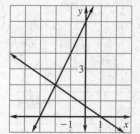

10. $3x - 2y = 16$
$5x + y = 18$

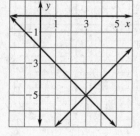

11. $2x - y = -13$
$y + 3x = -12$

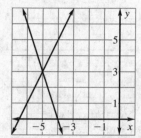

12. $6x + 2y = 8$
$-3x + 4y = 16$

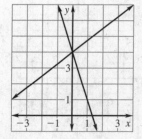

LESSON 7.1 **Practice** *continued*
For use with pages 375–382

Solve the linear system by graphing. Check your solution.

13. $y = 3x$
$y = 4x - 1$

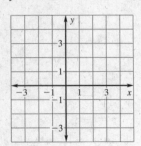

14. $2x + y = -4$
$x - y = -8$

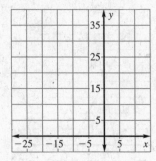

15. $-3x - y = -1$
$2x + 4y = -16$

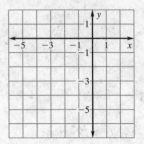

16. $2x + 2y = -6$
$-5x + y = 15$

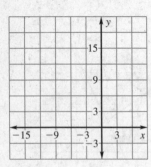

17. $-6x + y = 33$
$2x - 8y = -34$

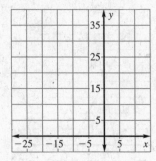

18. $-9x + 6y = -6$
$2x - 3y = 8$

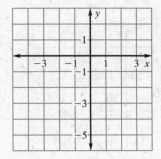

19. $3x + 2y = 3$
$5x + y = -9$

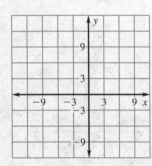

20. $x - y = 9$
$3x + 2y = 2$

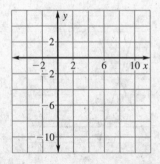

21. $6x + y = 19$
$5x - 2y = -4$

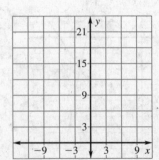

LESSON 7.1

Practice *continued*
For use with pages 375–382

22. Hanging Flower Baskets You will be making hanging flower baskets. The plants you have picked out are blooming annuals and non-blooming annuals. The blooming annuals cost $3.20 each and the non-blooming annuals cost $1.50 each. You bought a total of 24 plants for $49.60. Write a linear system of equations that you can use to find how many of each type of plant you bought. Then graph the linear system and use the graph to find how many of each type of plant you bought.

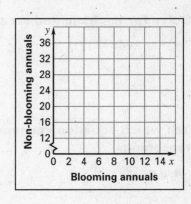

23. Baseball Outs In a game, 12 of a baseball team's 27 outs were fly balls. Twenty-five percent of the outs made by infielders and 100% of the outs made by outfielders were fly balls.

a. Write a linear system you can use to find the number of outs made by infielders and the number of outs made by outfielders. (*Hint:* Write one equation for the total number of outs and another equation for the number of fly ball outs.)

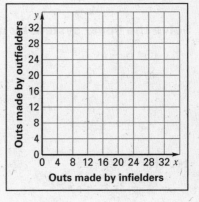

b. Graph your linear system.

c. How many outs were made by infielders? How many outs were made by outfielders?

Name _____   Date _____

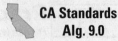

CA Standards
Alg. 9.0

Solve for the indicated variable.

1. $8x + 4y = 12; y$ **2.** $3x - 4y = 12; y$ **3.** $6x - 4y = 8; x$

Tell which equation you would use to isolate a variable. *Explain* your reasoning.

4. $x = 8y - 3$
$3x - 4y = 1$

5. $-4x + 5y = 11$
$y = 4x - 1$

6. $9 - 3x = y$
$3x - y = -2$

Solve the linear system by using substitution.

7. $x = 6 - 4y$
$2x - 3y = 1$

8. $4x + 3y = 0$
$2x + y = -2$

9. $-x + 2y = -6$
$8x + y = 31$

10. $6x - y = -35$
$5x - 2y = -35$

11. $-x + 3y = -9$
$8x - 4y = 32$

12. $3x + 3y = -18$
$4x - y = -14$

13. $2x + 2y = 6$
$-3x + 5y = -33$

14. $5x + 2y = 43$
$-6x + 3y = -30$

15. $4x - 2y = -4$
$7x - 5y = -19$

16. $3x + 2y = 5$
$5x - 9y = -4$

17. $4x - 3y = 28$
$2x + 3y = -4$

18. $8x + 8y = 24$
$x + 5y = 11$

LESSON 7.2

Practice _continued_
For use with pages 383–388

19. Drum Sticks A drummer is stocking up on drum sticks and brushes. The wood sticks that he buys are $10.50 a pair and the brushes are $24 a pair. He ends up spending $90 on sticks and brushes and buys two times as many pairs of sticks as brushes. How many pairs of sticks and brushes did he buy?

20. Mowing and Shoveling Last year you mowed grass and shoveled snow for 12 households. You earned $225 for mowing a household's lawn for the entire year and you earned $200 for shoveling a household's walk and driveway for an entire year. You earned a total of $2600 last year.

  a. Let x be the number of households you mowed for and let y be the number of households you shoveled for. Write an equation in x and y that shows the total number of households you worked for. Then write an equation in x and y that shows the total amount of money you earned.

  b. How many households did you mow the lawn for and how many households did you shovel the walk and driveway for?

21. Dimensions of a Metal Sheet A rectangular hole 3 centimeters wide and x centimeters long is cut in a rectangular sheet of metal that is 4 centimeters wide and y centimeters long. The length of the hole is 1 centimeter less than the length of the metal sheet. After the hole is cut, the area of the remaining metal sheet is 20 square centimeters. Find the length of the hole and the length of the metal sheet.

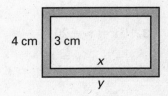

Rewrite the linear system so that the like terms are arranged in columns.

1. $8x - y = 19$
$y + 3x = 7$

2. $4x = y - 11$
$6y + 4x = -3$

3. $9x - 2y = 5$
$2y = -11x + 8$

Describe the first step you would use to solve the linear system.

4. $22x - y = -4$
$y = 6x - 5$

5. $25 = x - 7y$
$x + 12y = -8$

6. $3x + 7 = 2y$
$-2y - 1 = 10x$

7. $x + 9y = 2$
$14x - 9y = -4$

8. $4x + 3y = -6$
$3y = -5x + 1$

9. $4x + y = -10$
$x + y = -14$

Solve the linear system by using elimination.

10. $x + 5y = 28$
$-x - 2y = -13$

11. $7x - 4y = -30$
$3x + 4y = 10$

12. $6x + y = 39$
$-2x + y = -17$

13. $3x = y - 20$
$-7x - y = 40$

14. $2x - 6y = -10$
$4x = 10 + 6y$

15. $x - 3y = 6$
$-2x = 3y + 33$

16. $-3x = y - 20$
$-y = -5x + 4$

17. $x - \frac{1}{2}y = \frac{11}{2}$
$-x + 4y = 26$

18. $-\frac{2}{3}x + 6y = 38$
$x - 6y = -33$

19. $\frac{3}{2}x + y = -\frac{5}{2}$
$4x + y = -5$

20. $7x - \frac{1}{3}y = -29$
$2x - \frac{1}{3}y = -9$

21. $\frac{1}{2}x - \frac{3}{2}y = -\frac{29}{2}$
$-\frac{1}{2}x + 3y = 33$

LESSON 7.3

Practice continued
For use with pages 390–397

22. School Supplies You spend $2.75 to buy 3 folders and 2 packages of notebook paper from the school store. Your friend spends $3.25 to buy 5 folders and 2 packages of notebook paper. Find the cost of one folder and the cost of one package of notebook paper.

23. Spaghetti Dinner Your family attends the football booster's spaghetti dinner and pays $28 for 2 adults and 2 children. Another family pays $24 for 1 adult and 3 children. Find the cost of an adult's dinner and the cost of a child's dinner.

24. Floor Sander Rental A rental company charges a flat fee of x dollars for a floor sander rental plus y dollars per hour of the rental. One customer rents a floor sander for 4 hours and pays $63. Another customer rents a floor sander for 6 hours and pays $87.

a. Find the flat fee and the cost per hour for the rental.

b. How much would it cost someone to rent a sander for 11 hours?

Name _____ Date _____

Practice
For use with pages 398–404

Describe the first step you would use to solve the linear system.

1. $3x - 4y = 7$
$5x + 8y = 10$

2. $9x + 4y = 13$
$3x + 5y = 9$

3. $5x + 7y = -3$
$15x + 4y = -5$

4. $7x - 4y = 6$
$3x - 2y = -15$

5. $7x + 9y = -6$
$-5x + 14y = 11$

6. $9x - 5y = 14$
$-6x + 8y = 13$

Solve the linear system by using elimination.

7. $x + 3y = 1$
$-5x + 4y = -24$

8. $-3x - y = -15$
$8x + 4y = 48$

9. $x + 7y = -37$
$2x - 5y = 21$

10. $8x - 4y = -76$
$5x + 2y = -16$

11. $-3x + 10y = 23$
$5x + 2y = 55$

12. $9x - 4y = 26$
$18x + 7y = 22$

13. $4x - 3y = 16$
$16x + 10y = 240$

14. $20x + 10y = 100$
$-5x + 4y = 53$

15. $3x - 10y = -25$
$5x - 20y = -55$

16. $-3x - 4y = 27$
$5x - 6y = -7$

17. $2x + 7y = 2$
$5x - 2y = 83$

18. $3x - 5y = -16$
$2x - 3y = -8$

LESSON
7.4

Practice *continued*
For use with pages 398–404

19. Hockey Game Two families go to a hockey game. One family purchases two adult tickets and four youth tickets for $28. Another family purchases four adult tickets and five youth tickets for $45.50. Let *x* represent the cost in dollars of one adult ticket and let *y* represent the cost in dollars of one youth ticket.

   a. Write a linear system that represents this situation.

   b. Solve the linear system to find the cost of one adult and one youth ticket.

   c. How much would it cost two adults and five youths to attend the game?

20. Travel Agency A travel agency offers two Chicago outings. Plan A includes hotel accommodations for three nights and two pairs of baseball tickets worth a total of $557. Plan B includes hotel accommodations for five nights and four pairs of baseball tickets worth a total of $974. Let *x* represent the cost in dollars of one night's hotel accommodations and let *y* represent the cost in dollars of one pair of baseball tickets.

   a. Write a linear system you could use to find the cost of one night's hotel accommodations and the cost of one pair of baseball tickets.

   b. Solve the linear system to find the cost of one night's hotel accommodations and the cost of one pair of baseball tickets.

21. Highway Project There are fifteen workers employed on a highway project, some at $180 per day and some at $155 per day. The daily payroll is $2400. Let *x* represent the number of $180 per day workers and let *y* represent the number of $155 per day workers. Write and solve a linear system to find the number of workers employed at each wage.

LESSON 7.5 **Practice**
For use with pages 405–411

CA Standards
Alg. 9.0

Match the linear system with its graph. Then use the graph to tell whether the linear system has *one solution*, *no solution*, or *infinitely many solutions*.

1. $y + 3 = 4x$
$3y = 12x - 9$

2. $2x + y = 1$
$2x + y = 5$

3. $3x + y = 1$
$-2x + y = -3$

A.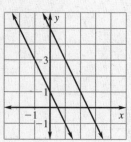

B.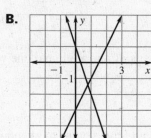

C.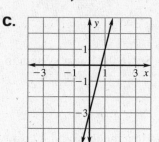

Graph the linear system. Then use the graph to tell whether the linear system has *one solution*, *no solution*, or *infinitely many solutions*.

4. $-6x + 2y = -2$
$-3x + y = 2$

5. $2y - x = -4$
$2x + y = 3$

6. $4x - y = 2$
$-x + 3y = 9$

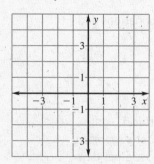

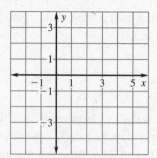

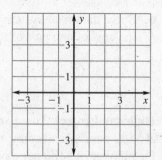

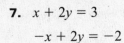

Practice *continued*
For use with pages 405–411

7. $x + 2y = 3$
$-x + 2y = -2$

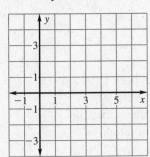

8. $3x + y = 4$
$x + \frac{1}{3}y = 2$

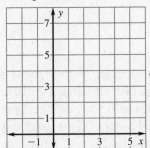

9. $2x - y = 4$
$-2x + y = -4$

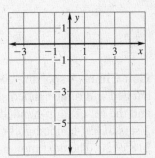

Solve the linear system by using substitution or elimination.

10. $3x - 2y = 24$
$x + 2y = 8$

11. $3x + 2y = 4$
$-6x - 4y = -8$

12. $x + y = 50$
$-3x + 2y = 0$

13. $-x + 4y = -3$
$-3x + 2y = 1$

14. $-x + 3y = 9$
$2x + y = 10$

15. $2x + y = 6$
$2x + y = -7$

Without solving the linear system, tell whether the linear system has *one solution, no solution,* or *infinitely many solutions.*

16. $-6x + 6y = -4$
$2x - 2y = 5$

17. $y + 2x = \frac{8}{3}$
$2x + y = -10$

18. $4x + 3y = 9$
$\frac{3}{4}x + y = 3$

19. $4x - 6y = -1$
$-\frac{3}{2}x + y = \frac{1}{4}$

20. $-\frac{2}{3}x + y = 2$
$-6x + 3y = 6$

21. $9x - 15y = 15$
$x + \frac{3}{5}y = 1$

LESSON 7.5

Practice *continued*
For use with pages 405–411

22. $-3x + 4y = 2$

$2y = \dfrac{3}{2}x + 1$

23. $3x + y = 4$

$x + \dfrac{1}{3}y = 2$

24. $-4x + 3y = 2$

$4 - 6y = -8x$

25. **Golf Clubs** A sporting goods store stocks a "better" set of golf clubs in both left-handed and right-handed sets. The set of left-handed golf clubs sells for x dollars and the set of right-handed golf clubs sells for y dollars. In one month, the store sells 2 sets of left-handed golf clubs and 12 sets of right-handed golf clubs for a total of $1859.30. The next month, the store sells 2 sets of left-handed golf clubs and 22 sets of right-handed golf clubs for a total of $3158.80. Is there enough information to determine the cost of each kind of set? *Explain.*

26. **Comedy Tickets** The table below shows the ticket sales at an all-ages comedy club on a Friday night and a Saturday night.

Day	Number of adult tickets	Number of student tickets	Total sales (dollars)
Friday	30	20	910
Saturday	45	30	1365

a. Let x represent the cost (in dollars) of one adult ticket and let y represent the cost (in dollars) of one student ticket. Write a linear system that models the situation.

b. Solve the linear system.

c. Can you determine how much each kind of ticket costs? Why or why not?

Name _____   Date _____

Find the distance _d_ for the given rate _r_ and time _t_.

1. $r = 36$ m/min; $t = 2$ min

2. $r = 65$ mi/h; $t = 8$ h

3. $r = 45$ km/h; $t = 3$ h

4. $r = 30$ ft/sec; $t = 300$ sec

Find the rate _r_ for the given distance _d_ and time _t_.

5. $d = 75{,}000$ mi; $t = 5$ yr

6. $d = 3200$ km; $t = 4$ days

7. $d = 720$ in.; $t = 20$ sec

8. $d = 7.5$ mi; $t = 15$ days

Find the time _t_ for the given distance _d_ and rate _r_.

9. $d = 4$ m; $r = 1$ m/yr

10. $d = 21$ km; $r = 6$ km/h

11. $d = 1875$ cm; $r = 125$ cm/sec

12. $d = 6$ mi; $r = 0.25$ mi/min

13. Canoeing A canoe is traveling on a river. Let r be the rate (in kilometers per hour) of the canoe in still water, and let c be the rate (in kilometers per hour) of the current. Use r and c to write an equation for the statement.

a. The rate of the canoe going with the current is 6 kilometers per hour.

b. The rate of the canoe going against the current is 3 kilometers per hour.

LESSON 7.6

Practice *continued*
For use with pages 413–417

14. Walking You leave school at the end of the day and walk home at a leisurely pace of 2 miles per hour. You sister leaves school 15 minutes later and walks at a pace of 3 miles per hour.

    a. How long will it take for your sister to catch up with you?

    b. Is there enough information to determine who arrives home first?

15. Fishing Barge A fishing barge leaves from a dock and moves upstream (against the current) at a rate of 3.8 miles per hour until it reaches its destination. After the people on the barge are done fishing, the barge moves the same distance downstream (with the current) at a rate of 8 miles per hour until it returns to the dock. The speed of the current remains constant. Use the models below to write and solve a system of equations to find the average speed of the barge in still water, and the speed of the current.

Upstream: Speed of barge in still water − Speed of current = Speed of barge
Downstream: Speed of barge in still water + Speed of current = Speed of barge

Name _____   Date _____

Find the unit cost given the total cost *C* and the amount *a*.

1. $C = \$15.00$, $a = 2$ lb

2. $C = \$24.00$, $a = 6$ gal

3. $C = \$32.40$, $a = 24$ g

4. $C = \$6.50$, $a = 25$ oz

5. $C = \$40.00$, $a = 32$ mg

6. $C = \$60.90$, $a = 42$ mL

Find the percent of a component in a mixture given the amount *c* of the component and the amount *m* of the mixture.

7. $c = 20$ gal, $m = 100$ gal

8. $c = 3$ L, $m = 20$ L

9. $c = 17$ mg, $m = 25$ mg

10. $c = 30$ pt, $m = 120$ pt

11. $c = 3.5$ qt, $m = 28$ qt

12. $c = 0.9$ g, $m = 37.5$ g

Find the amount of the component in a solution given the amount of the solution and the percent of the component.

13. 6 gallons of a 75% antifreeze solution

14. 4 liters of a 10% acid solution

15. 15 milliliters of a 25% ethanol solution

16. 20 pints of a 5% saline solution

17. **Food** You are preparing a snack mix of raisins and peanuts for a group of hikers. Raisins are $4.00 per pound and peanuts are $3.25 per pound. You want to make 5 pounds of snack mix for a cost of $3.40 per pound.

   a. Write a linear system that can be used to determine how many pounds of raisins and peanuts you should mix.

   b. Solve the linear system from part (a).

LESSON 7.7

18. **Fruit Juice** A pitcher contains 64 ounces of a fruit juice which is 10% apple juice. Eight ounces of 100% apple juice are added to the pitcher. What percent of the juice in the pitcher is apple juice?

19. **Beading** A crafts store is packaging round beads and bugle beads together. The table shows the retail price of the beads when packaged separately.

Type of bead	Size of package	Price per package
Round	7.5 grams	$2.17
Bugle	35 grams	$3.24

a. Find the unit cost of the round bead and the unit cost of the bugle bead.

b. Write a linear system that can be used to determine how many grams of round beads and bugle beads should be in a 10 gram package that sells for $2.50.

c. Solve the linear system from part (b).

d. Write and solve a linear system to find how many grams of round beads and bugle beads should be in a 10 gram package that sells for $.80.

Name _____ Date _____

LESSON
7.8
Practice
For use with pages 424–432

CA Standards
Alg. 6.0

LESSON 7.8

Tell whether the ordered pair is a solution of the inequality.

1. $x + y > -9; (0, 0)$

2. $x - y \geq 8; (14, 9)$

3. $2x - y > 4; (-6, -15)$

4. $2x + y > -5; (-5, 12)$

5. $5x + 2y \leq 8; (-3, 6)$

6. $4x - 3y \geq -5; (6, 8)$

7. $0.5x + 2.5y \geq 2; (0, 0)$

8. $1.2x - 3.1y < 4; (3, -1)$

9. $0.2y - 0.5x > -1; (-4, -8)$

Graph the inequality.

10. $y - x < 6$

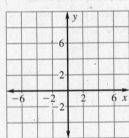

11. $x - y > -4$

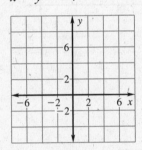

12. $2y - x < 2$

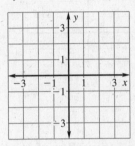

13. $4y \leq 6x - 2$

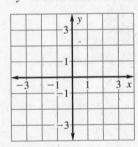

14. $5y \leq 10x + 15$

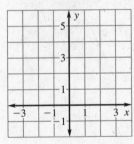

15. $6y + 3 \geq -18x$

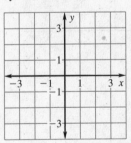

LESSON 7.8 Practice continued
For use with pages 424–432

16. $2(y + 3) < 4x$

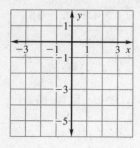

17. $2y - 3x \geq -8$

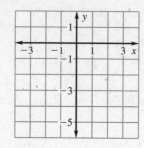

18. $2(x - y) < -5$

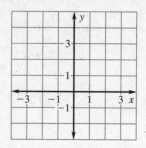

19. $y > 7$

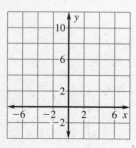

20. $x \leq -5$

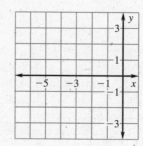

21. $y < -4$

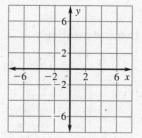

Write an inequality of the graph shown.

22.

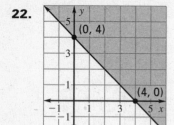

23.

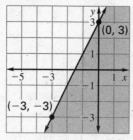

24.

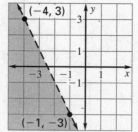

LESSON 7.8 **Practice** *continued*
For use with pages 424–432

25. Clothes You are going clothes shopping and can spend at most $130 on clothes. It costs $30 for a pair of pants and $22 for a shirt. Let x represent the number of pants you can buy. Let y represent the number of shirts you can buy.

   a. Write and graph an inequality that describes the different number of shirts and pants you can buy.

   b. Give three possible combinations of pants and shirts that you can buy.

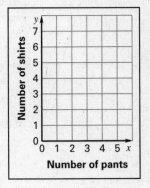

26. Window The area of the window shown is less than 42 square feet. Let x and y represent the heights of the triangular and rectangular portions of the window, respectively.

   a. Write and graph an inequality that describes the different dimensions of the window.

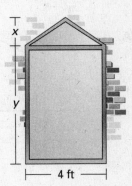

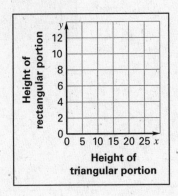

   b. Could the height of the triangular portion be 2 feet and the height of the rectangular portion be 8 feet?

LESSON 7.9 **Practice**
For use with pages 433–440

CA Standards
Alg. 9.0

Tell whether the ordered pair is a solution of the system of inequalities.

1. $(3, 0)$

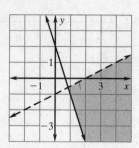

2. $(2, 2)$

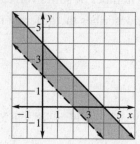

3. $(-2, 2)$

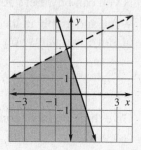

Match the system of inequalities with its graph.

4. $\frac{1}{2}x + y \geq 3$

$x > -1$

5. $y - \frac{1}{2}x \leq 3$

$x < -1$

6. $y \leq \frac{1}{2}x + 3$

$x > -1$

A.

B.

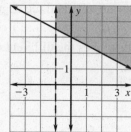

C.

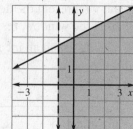

Graph the system of inequalities.

7. $x > -1$

$x < 1$

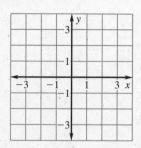

8. $y \geq 2$

$y < 3$

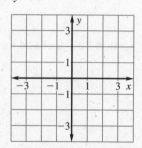

9. $x + y > 1$

$x \leq y$

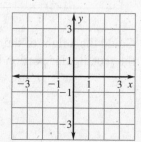

California Math, Algebra 1
Chapter 7 Practice Workbook

LESSON 7.9

Practice *continued*
For use with pages 433–440

10. $x \geq y + 2$

$2x + y < 4$

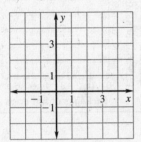

11. $y \geq 2$

$x + y \leq -3$

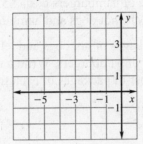

12. $x \leq -y$

$2x - y < 4$

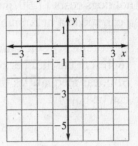

Write a system of inequalities for the shaded region.

13.

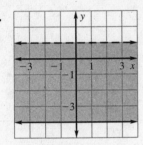

14.

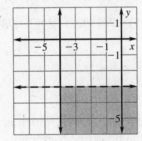

15.

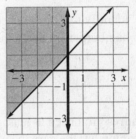

16.

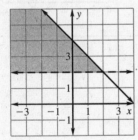

17.

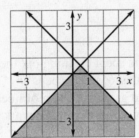

18.

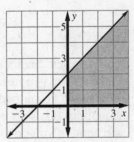

Name _____ Date _____

19. Cookout You are planning a cookout. You figure that you will need at least 5 packages of hot dogs and hamburgers. A package of hot dogs costs $1.90 and a package of hamburgers costs $5.20. You can spend a maximum of $20 on the hot dogs and hamburgers.

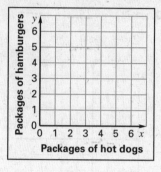

a. Let x represent the number of packages of hot dogs and let y represent the number of packages of hamburgers. Write a system of linear inequalities for the number of packages of each that can be bought.

b. Graph the system of inequalities.

c. Identify two possible combinations of packages of hot dogs and hamburgers you can buy.

20. Chores You need at least 4 hours to do your chores, which is cleaning out the garage and weeding the flower beds around your house. It is 1:30 P.M. on Sunday and your friend wants you to go to the movies at 7:00 P.M.

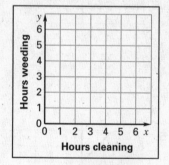

a. How much time do you have between now and 7:00 P.M. to do your chores?

b. Let x represent the number of hours spent cleaning out the garage and let y represent the number of hours spent on weeding the flower beds. Write and graph a system of linear inequalities that shows the number of hours you can work on each chore if you go to the movies.

c. Identify two possible combinations of time you can spend on each chore.

Practice
For use with pages 467–473

Simplify the expression. Write your answer using exponents.

1. $\dfrac{6^{14}}{6^8}$

2. $\dfrac{14^5}{14^4}$

3. $\dfrac{(-5)^7}{(-5)^2}$

4. $\dfrac{12^5 \cdot 12^3}{12^4}$

5. $\dfrac{8^{17}}{8^3 \cdot 8^7}$

6. $\left(\dfrac{3}{4}\right)^5$

7. $\left(-\dfrac{1}{5}\right)^6$

8. $3^8 \cdot \dfrac{1}{3^1}$

9. $\left(\dfrac{1}{4}\right)^5 \cdot 4^{13}$

Simplify the expression.

10. $\dfrac{1}{y^9} \cdot y^{15}$

11. $z^{16} \cdot \dfrac{1}{z^7}$

12. $\left(\dfrac{a}{b}\right)^8$

13. $\left(-\dfrac{6}{z}\right)^3$

14. $\left(\dfrac{a^3}{2b^5}\right)^4$

15. $\left(\dfrac{3x^4}{y^6}\right)^5$

16. $\left(\dfrac{m^4}{5n^9}\right)^3$

17. $\left(\dfrac{3x^7}{2y^{12}}\right)^4$

18. $\left(\dfrac{2m^5}{3n^9}\right)^5$

19. Area The area of New Zealand is 104,454 square miles and the area of Saint Kitts and Nevis, islands in the Caribbean Sea, is 104 square miles. Use order of magnitude to estimate how many times greater New Zealand's area is than Saint Kitts and Nevis' area.

Practice *continued*
For use with pages 467–473

20. Cell Phone Subscribers The table below shows the approximate number of cell phone subscribers in selected countries in 2003.

Country	Dominican Republic	Poland	Solomon Islands
Number of subscribers	10^6	10^7	10^3

   a. How many times greater is the number of cell phone subscribers in Poland than in the Solomon Islands?

   b. How many times greater is the number of cell phone subscribers in the Dominican Republic than in the Solomon Islands?

21. Glass Vase You are taking a glass-blowing class and have created a vase in the shape of a sphere. The vase will have a hole in the top so you can put flowers in it and it will sit on a stand. The radius of your vase is $\frac{21}{2}$ inches. Use the formula $V = \frac{4}{3}\pi r^3$ to write an expression for the volume of your vase.

LESSON 8.2

LESSON
8.3
Practice
For use with pages 474–480

CA Standards
Alg. 2.0

Evaluate the expression.

1. 3^{-5}

2. 10^{-3}

3. $(-2)^{-6}$

4. 5^0

5. $(-6)^0$

6. $\left(\frac{4}{3}\right)^0$

7. $\left(\frac{5}{8}\right)^{-2}$

8. $\left(\frac{7}{4}\right)^3$

9. 0^{-5}

10. $10^{-2} \cdot 10^{-3}$

11. $4^{-6} \cdot 4^3$

12. $\frac{1}{5^{-4}}$

Simplify the expression. Write your answer using only positive exponent

13. x^{-7}

14. $6y^{-4}$

15. $(2$

16. $(-3m)^{-4}$

17. $a^2 b^{-4}$

18. $3x^{-2}y^{-5}$

19. $(4x^{-4}y^2)^{-3}$

20. $(8mn^3)^0$

21. $\frac{c^{-3}}{d^{-5}}$

22. $\frac{x^2}{y^{-4}}$

23. $\frac{x^{-6}}{4y^5}$

24. $\frac{1}{3x^{-3}y^{-7}}$

Practice *continued*
For use with pages 474–480

25. Paper A sheet of 67-pound paper has a thickness of 100^{-1} inch.

    a. Write and evaluate an expression for the total thickness of 5 sheets of 67-pound paper.

    b. Write and evaluate an expression for the total thickness of 2^3 sheets of 67-pound paper.

26. Frogs A frog egg currently has a radius of 5^{-1} centimeter. Write an expression using positive exponents for the volume of the frog egg. Use the formula for the volume of a sphere $V = \frac{4}{3}\pi r^3$.

27. Metric System The metric system has names for very small lengths.

    a. One micrometer is 10^3 times the length of one nanometer. One nanometer is 10^{-9} meter. Write one micrometer in meters.

    b. One femtometer is 10^3 times the length of one attometer. One attometer is 10^{-18} meter. Write one femtometer in meters.

    c. One centimeter is 10^{10} times the length of one picometer. One picometer is 10^{-12} meter. Write one centimeter in meters.

LESSON 8.3

Practice
For use with pages 482–490

CA Standards
Alg. 1.0
Alg. 25.1

Simplify the expression.

1. $\sqrt{200}$

2. $\sqrt{45}$

3. $\sqrt{112}$

4. $\sqrt{400d}$

5. $\sqrt{9y^2}$

6. $\sqrt{25n^3}$

7. $\sqrt{3} \cdot \sqrt{21}$

8. $\sqrt{20} \cdot \sqrt{15}$

9. $\sqrt{10x} \cdot \sqrt{2x}$

10. $\sqrt{\dfrac{16}{81}}$

11. $\sqrt{\dfrac{5}{49}}$

12. $\sqrt{\dfrac{x^2}{144}}$

Simplify the expression by rationalizing the denominator.

13. $\dfrac{4}{\sqrt{5}}$

14. $\sqrt{\dfrac{3}{50}}$

15. $\sqrt{\dfrac{9}{75}}$

16. $\dfrac{2}{\sqrt{p}}$

17. $\dfrac{1}{\sqrt{3y}}$

18. $\dfrac{9}{\sqrt{2x}}$

Simplify the expression.

19. $10\sqrt{7} + 3\sqrt{7}$

20. $4\sqrt{5} - 7\sqrt{5}$

21. $\sqrt{7}(4 - \sqrt{7})$

22. $\sqrt{5}(8\sqrt{10} + 1)$

23. $(2\sqrt{3} + 5)^2$

24. $(6 + \sqrt{3})(6 - \sqrt{3})$

LESSON 8.4 **Practice** *continued*
For use with pages 482–490

25. Water Flow You can measure the speed of water by using an L-shaped tube. The speed V of the water (in miles per hour) is given by the function $V = \sqrt{\frac{5}{2}h}$ where h is the height of the column of water above the surface (in inches).

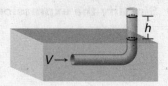

a. If you use the tube in a river and find that h is 6 inches, what is the speed of the water? Round your answer to the nearest hundredth.

b. If you use the tube in a river and find that h is 8.5 inches, what is the speed of the water? Round your answer to the nearest hundredth.

26. Walking Speed The maximum walking speed S (in feet per second) of an animal is given by the function $S = \sqrt{gL}$ where g is 32 feet per second squared and L is the length of the animal's leg (in feet).

a. How fast can an animal whose legs are 9 inches long walk? Round your answer to the nearest hundredth.

b. How fast can an animal whose legs are 3 feet long walk? Round your answer to the nearest hundredth.

LESSON 8.5 Practice
For use with pages 491–496

CA Standards
Gr. 7 MG 3.3

Let *a* and *b* represent the lengths of the legs of a right triangle, and let *c* represent the length of the hypotenuse. Find the unknown length.

1. $a = 1, b = 5$

2. $b = 4, c = 9$

3. $a = 6, b = 6$

4. $b = 7, c = 12$

5. $a = 2, b = 8$

6. $a = 6, b = 30$

7. $a = 4, b = 15$

8. $b = 7, c = 11$

9. $a = 10, b = 20$

10. $a = 30, b = 40$

11. $a = 15, c = 25$

12. $a = 11, b = 22$

Given that *D* is the midpoint of segment *AC*, find the unknown length. Round your answer to the nearest tenth, if necessary.

13.

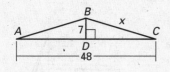

14.

15.

Tell whether the triangle with the given side lengths is a right triangle.

16. $4, 5, 6$

17. $15, 20, 25$

18. $9, 15, 20$

LESSON 8.5

LESSON 8.5

Practice *continued*
For use with pages 491–496

19. **Shuffleboard** The playing bed of a shuffleboard table is in the shape of a rectangle. If the playing bed measures 154 inches by 20 inches, what is the length of the diagonal from one corner of the playing bed to the opposite corner? Round your answer to the nearest inch.

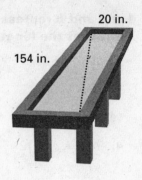

20. **Indirect Measurement** You are trying to determine the distance across a pond. You put posts into the ground at *A*, *B*, and *C* so that angle *B* is a right angle. You measure and find that the length of *AB* is 18 feet and the length of *CB* is 28 feet. How wide is the pond from *A* to *C*? Round your answer to the nearest foot.

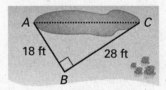

21. **Badminton** You are setting up a badminton net. To keep each pole standing straight, you use two ropes and two stakes as shown. How long is each piece of rope? Round your answer to the nearest tenth.

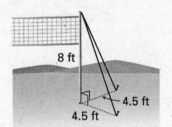

LESSON 8.6 **Practice**
For use with pages 498–503

CA Standards
Alg. 2.0

Evaluate the expression.

1. $\sqrt[3]{343}$

2. $\sqrt[3]{-27}$

3. $\sqrt[3]{1728}$

4. $-\sqrt[3]{1}$

5. $-\sqrt[3]{125} + \sqrt[3]{729}$

6. $\sqrt{64} - \sqrt[3]{64}$

7. $\sqrt[3]{8} + \sqrt{9}$

8. $\sqrt[3]{-216} - \sqrt{49}$

9. Describe and correct the error in evaluating the expresions.

$$\sqrt[3]{64} + \sqrt{121} = 8 + 11$$
$$= 19$$

Evaluate the expression.

10. $81^{1/2}$

11. $64^{1/3}$

12. $25^{-1/2}$

13. $36^{5/2}$

14. $343^{4/3}$

15. $8^{-5/3}$

16. $16^{-3/2}$

17. $125^{-4/3}$

Simplify the expression. Write your answer using only positive exponents.

18. $27^{1/3} \cdot 27^{-4/3}$

19. $x^{3/2} \cdot x^{5/2}$

20. $\left(\dfrac{8}{125}\right)^{2/3} \cdot \left(\dfrac{8}{125}\right)^{1/3}$

21. $\dfrac{x^{-5/3}\left(\sqrt[3]{x}\right)^4}{x^{1/3}}$

22. $\dfrac{49^{1/2}}{49^{-5/2} \cdot 49^{3/2}}$

23. $x^{-1/3} \cdot \dfrac{x^{7/3}}{\left(x^{-5}\right)^{-1/3}}$

LESSON 8.6

24. **Snow Globe** You bought a snow globe for your friend and you want to wrap the gift in its cubical box. Use the formula $S = 6V^{2/3}$, where V is the volume of the cube, to find the surgace area S of the box.

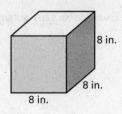

25. **Cliff** A stone is dropped from the top of a cliff. The cliff is 100 feet high. use the formula $t = \dfrac{h^{1/2}}{4}$, where h is the height of the cliff, to find the amount of time t (in seconds) that it takes for the stone to reach the ground below the cliff.

26. **Beach Ball** The radius r of a sphere can be approximated by the formula $r = \dfrac{(3V)^{1/3}}{2.3}$. To the nearest tenth of a foot, approximate the radius of a beach ball with a volume of 9 cubic feet.

LESSON 8.6

LESSON 9.1 Practice
For use with pages 519–526

CA Standards
Alg. 10.0

Write the polynomial so that the exponents decrease from left to right. Identify the degree and leading coefficient of the polynomial.

1. $4n^5$

2. $4x - 2x^2 + 3$

3. $6y^3 - 2y^2 + 4y^4 - 5$

Tell whether the expression is a polynomial. If it is a polynomial, find its degree and classify it by the number of its terms. Otherwise, tell why it is not a polynomial.

4. 10^x

5. $-6n^2 - n^3 + 4$

6. $w^{-3} + 5$

Find the sum or difference.

7. $13xy - 9xy$

8. $-7cd^2 + 3cd^2$

9. $(3z^2 + z - 4) + (2z^2 + 2z - 3)$

10. $(8c^2 - 4c + 1) + (-3c^2 + c + 5)$

11. $(2x^2 + 5x - 1) + (x^2 - 5x + 7)$

12. $(10b^2 - 3b + 2) - (4b^2 + 5b + 1)$

13. $(-4m^2 + 3m - 1) - (m + 2)$

14. $(3m + 4) - (2m^2 - 6m + 5)$

Write a polynomial that represents the perimeter of the figure.

15.

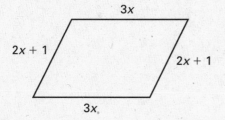

16.

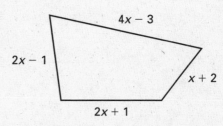

LESSON 9.1

17. Floor Plan The first floor of a home has the floor plan shown.
Write a polynomial that represents the area of the first floor.

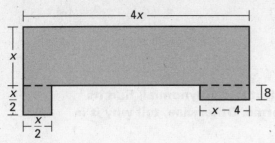

18. Profit For 1995 through 2005, the revenue R (in dollars) and the
cost C (in dollars) of producing a product can be modeled by

$$R = \frac{1}{4}t^2 + \frac{21}{4}t + 400 \quad \text{and} \quad C = \frac{1}{12}t^2 + \frac{13}{4}t + 200$$

where t is the number of years since 1995. Write an
equation for the profit P earned from 1995 to 2005.
(*Hint:* Profit = Revenue − Cost)

LESSON 9.2 **Practice**
For use with pages 527–533

Find the product.

1. $3x^2(7x)$

2. $z^2(-8z^5)$

3. $-4b^2(-9b^5)$

4. $x^2(6x^2 - 3x - 1)$

5. $-5a^3(4a^4 - 3a + 1)$

6. $4d^2(-2d^3 + 5d^2 - 6d + 2)$

7. $(3x + 1)(2x - 5)$

8. $(2y + 3)(y - 5)$

9. $(6a - 3)(4a - 1)$

10. $(b - 8)(5b - 2)$

11. $(8m + 7)(2m + 3)$

12. $(-p + 2)(3p^2 + 1)$

13. $(2z - 7)(-z + 3)$

14. $(-3d + 10)(2d - 1)$

15. $(n + 1)(n^2 + 4n + 5)$

16. $(w - 3)(w^2 + 8w + 1)$

17. $(2s + 5)(s^2 + 3s - 1)$

18. $(x^2 - 4xy + y^2)(5xy)$

Simplify the expression.

19. $a(3a + 1) + (a + 1)(a - 1)$

20. $(x + 2)(x + 5) - x(4x - 1)$

21. $(m + 7)(m - 3) + (m - 4)(m + 5)$

22. $2y^2(y - 4) + (y + 3)(2y - 1)$

LESSON 9.2

Write a polynomial for the area of the shaded region.

23.

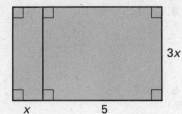

24.

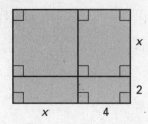

25. **Flower Bed** You are designing a rectangular flower bed
    that you will border using brick pavers. The width of the border
    around the bed will be the same on every side, as shown.

    a. Write a polynomial that represents the total area of
    the flower bed and the border.

    b. Find the total area of the flower bed and border when
    the width of the border is 1.5 feet.

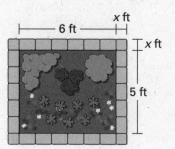

26. **School Enrollment** During the period 1995–2002, the number S of
    students (in thousands) enrolled in school in the U.S. and the percent
    P (in decimal form) of this amount that are between 7 and 13 years
    old can be modeled by

    $$S = 32.6t^3 - 376.45t^2 + 1624.2t + 66{,}939$$

    and

    $$P = 0.000005t^4 - 0.0003t^3 + 0.003t^2 - 0.007t + 0.4$$

    where t is the number of years since 1995.

    a. Find the values of S and P for $t = 0$. What does the product $S \cdot P$
    mean for $t = 0$ in the context of this problem?

    b. Write an equation that models the number N of students (in thousands)
    that are between 7 and 13 years old as a function of the number of
    years since 1995.

    c. How many students between 7 and 13 years old were enrolled in 1995?

LESSON 9.3

Practice
For use with pages 534–539

Find the product of the square of the binomial.

1. $(x - 9)^2$

2. $(m + 11)^2$

3. $(5s + 2)^2$

4. $(3m + 7)^2$

5. $(4p - 5)^2$

6. $(7a - 6)^2$

7. $(10z - 3)^2$

8. $(2x + y)^2$

9. $(3y - x)^2$

Find the product of the sum and difference.

10. $(a - 9)(a + 9)$

11. $(z - 20)(z + 20)$

12. $(5r + 1)(5r - 1)$

13. $(6m + 10)(6m - 10)$

14. $(7p - 2)(7p + 2)$

15. $(9c - 1)(9c + 1)$

16. $(4x + 3)(4x - 3)$

17. $(4 - w)(4 + w)$

18. $(5 - 2y)(5 + 2y)$

***Describe* how you can use mental math to find the product.**

19. $15 \cdot 25$

20. $43 \cdot 57$

21. 18^2

LESSON 9.3

Practice *continued*
For use with pages 534–539

22. **Prizes** You have a 25% chance of winning a stuffed animal while playing a game at a fair. What percent of the possible outcomes involve winning a stuffed animal at least once?

    A 43.75%   **B** 50%   **C** 56.25%   **D** 75%

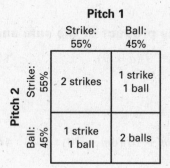

First Game

23. **Baseball Statistics** During a baseball game, 55% of the pitches thrown were strikes. The area model shows the possible outcomes of two pitches.

   a. What percent of the possible outcomes involve throwing exactly one strike? *Explain* how you found your answer using the area model.

   b. Show how you could use a polynomial to model the possible results of two pitches.

LESSON 9.4 Practice
For use with pages 540–547

CA Standards
Alg. 10.0

Divide.

1. $3x^3 \div (-15x)$

2. $-6y^5 \div y^2$

3. $42z^7 \div 6z^{12}$

4. $-7a^6 \div (-35a^7)$

5. $(18x^3 - 24x^2 + 12x) \div 6x$

6. $(-5x^3 + 15x^2 - 30x) \div (-5x)$

7. $(22x^4 - 18x^2 + 6x) \div (-2x)$

8. $(x^2 + 6x + 5) \div (x + 5)$

9. $(5x^2 + 7x - 6) \div (x + 2)$

10. $(4x^2 + x - 5) \div (x - 1)$

11. $(6x^2 + 22x - 8) \div (x + 4)$

12. $(4x^2 + x - 8) \div (x - 2)$

13. $(9x^2 + 5x - 6) \div (1 + x)$

14. $(3x^2 - 7x + 14) \div (2 + 3x)$

Find the value of k.

15. When $2x^2 + 3x + k$ is divided by $x + 1$, the remainder is 2.

16. When $36x^2 + k$ is divided by $6x + 3$, the remainder is 0.

LESSON 9.4 **Practice** *continued*
For use with pages 540–547

Divide the surface area of the rectangular prism by its volume.

17.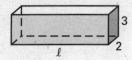
3
2
ℓ

18.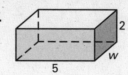
2
w
5

19. **Scootcar Rental** A resort area offers rentals of scootcars
(a cross between a scooter and a small car) for $40 per hour
plus a $4.50 gasoline fill-up fee. Write an equation that gives
the average cost C per hour as a function of the number h
of hours the scootcar is rented.

20. **Juice Bar** Between 1995 and 2004, the ratio R of the number of
drinks sold (in thousands) made from fruit juice to the total number
of drinks (in thousands) sold at a juice bar can be modeled by

$$R = \frac{2t + 16}{3t + 18}$$

where t is the number of years since 1995. Make a table for the model.
Describe how the ratio changed during this period.

LESSON
9.5

Practice
For use with pages 549–554

Solve the equation.

1. $(x + 14)(x - 3) = 0$

2. $(m - 12)(m + 5) = 0$

3. $(p + 15)(p + 24) = 0$

4. $(n - 8)(n - 9) = 0$

5. $(d + 8)\left(d - \dfrac{1}{2}\right) = 0$

6. $\left(c + \dfrac{3}{4}\right)(c - 6) = 0$

7. $(2z - 8)(z + 5) = 0$

8. $(y - 3)(5y + 10) = 0$

9. $(6b - 4)(b - 8) = 0$

10. $(8x + 4)(6x - 3) = 0$

11. $(3x + 9)(6x - 3) = 0$

12. $(4x + 5)(4x - 5) = 0$

Factor out the greatest common monomial factor.

13. $10x - 10y$

14. $8x^2 + 20y$

15. $18a^2 - 6b$

16. $4x^2 - 4x$

17. $r^2 + 2rs$

18. $2m^2 + 6mn$

19. $5p^2q + 10q$

20. $9a^5 + a^3$

21. $6w^3 - 14w^2$

Solve the equation.

22. $m^2 - 10m = 0$

23. $b^2 + 14b = 0$

24. $5w^2 - 5w = 0$

25. $24k^2 + 24k = 0$

26. $8r^2 - 24r = 0$

27. $9p^2 + 18p = 0$

LESSON 9.5

LESSON 9.5 **Practice** *continued*
For use with pages 549–554

28. $6n^2 - 15n = 0$ **29.** $-8y^2 - 10y = 0$ **30.** $-10b^2 + 25b = 0$

31. $8c^2 = 4c$ **32.** $30r^2 = -15r$ **33.** $-24y^2 = 9y$

Find the roots of the polynomial.

34. $5n^2 - 15n$ **35.** $8z^2 - 4z$ **36.** $2z^2 + 7z$

37. Diving Board A diver jumps from a diving board that is 24 feet above the water. The height of the diver is given by

$h = -16(t - 1.5)(t + 1)$

where the height h is measured in feet, and the time t is measured in seconds. When will the diver hit the water? Can you see a quick way to find the answer? *Explain.*

38. Dog To catch a frisbee, a dog leaps into the air with an initial velocity of 14 feet per second.

  a. Write a model for the height of the dog above the ground.

  b. After how many seconds does the dog land on the ground?

39. Desktop Areas You have two components to the desktop where you do your homework that fit together into an L shape. The two components have the same area.

  a. Write an equation that relates the areas of the desktop components.

  b. Find the value of w.

  c. What is the combined area of the desktop components?

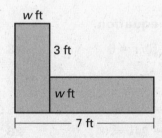

LESSON 9.6 **Practice**
For use with pages 555–562

CA Standards
Alg. 11.0
Alg. 14.0

Factor the trinomial.

1. $x^2 + 8x + 7$

2. $b^2 - 7b + 10$

3. $w^2 - 12w - 13$

4. $p^2 + 10p + 25$

5. $m^2 - 10m + 24$

6. $y^2 - 5y - 24$

7. $a^2 + 13a + 36$

8. $n^2 + 2n - 48$

9. $z^2 - 14z + 40$

Solve the equation.

10. $y^2 + 17y + 72 = 0$

11. $a^2 - 9a - 36 = 0$

12. $w^2 - 13w + 42 = 0$

13. $m^2 - 5m = 14$

14. $x^2 + 11x = -24$

15. $n^2 + 27 = 12n$

16. $d^2 + 5d = 50$

17. $p^2 + 48 = -16p$

18. $z^2 - 30 = z$

Find the roots of the polynomial.

19. $x^2 - 5x - 36$

20. $x^2 + 8x - 20$

21. $x^2 - 11x + 24$

22. $x^2 + 11x + 28$

23. $x^2 + 11x - 12$

24. $x^2 + 3x - 18$

LESSON 9.6

Name _____   Date _____

Solve the equation.

25. $x(x + 17) = -60$ **26.** $p(p - 4) = 32$ **27.** $w(w + 8) = -15$

28. $n(n + 6) = 7$ **29.** $s^2 - 3(s + 2) = 4$ **30.** $d^2 + 18(d + 4) = -9$

31. Patio Area A community center is building a patio area along two sides of its pool. The pool is rectangular with a width of 50 feet and a length of 100 feet. The patio area will have the same width on each side of the pool.

   a. Write a polynomial that represents the combined area of the pool and the patio area.

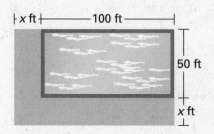

   b. The combined area of the pool and patio should be 8400 square feet. How wide should the patio area be?

32. Area Rug You are creating your own rug from a square piece of remnant carpeting. You plan on cutting 4 inches from the length and 3 inches from the width. The area of the resulting rug is 1056 square inches.

   a. Write a polynomial that represents the area of your rug.

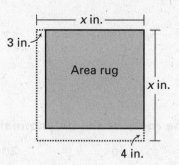

   b. What is the perimeter of the original piece of remnant carpeting?

LESSON 9.7 Practice
For use with pages 565–572

Factor the trinomial.

1. $-x^2 - 3x + 28$

2. $-p^2 + 8p - 12$

3. $-m^2 - 13m - 40$

4. $2y^2 + 15y + 7$

5. $3a^2 - 13a + 4$

6. $5d^2 - 18d - 8$

7. $6c^2 + 7c + 2$

8. $10n^2 - 26n + 12$

9. $12w^2 + 8w - 15$

10. $-2b^2 - 5b + 12$

11. $-3r^2 - 17r - 10$

12. $-4s^2 + 6s + 4$

Solve the equation.

13. $-x^2 + x + 20 = 0$

14. $-m^2 - 10m - 16 = 0$

15. $-p^2 + 13p - 42 = 0$

16. $2c^2 - 11c + 5 = 0$

17. $2y^2 + y - 10 = 0$

18. $16r^2 + 18r + 5 = 0$

19. $3w^2 + 19w + 6 = 0$

20. $12n^2 - 11n + 2 = 0$

21. $15a^2 - 2a - 8 = 0$

22. $-2x^2 - 9x - 4 = 0$

23. $-3s^2 - s + 10 = 0$

24. $8d^2 - 6d - 5 = 0$

Practice *continued*
For use with pages 565–572

Find the roots of the polynomial.

25. $-x^2 + 6x + 27$ **26.** $6x^2 + 45x - 24$ **27.** $-3x^2 - 14x + 24$

28. $-2x^2 + 2x + 4$ **29.** $3x^2 - 17x + 20$ **30.** $8x^2 + 53x - 21$

31. $4x^2 + 29x + 30$ **32.** $-2x^2 - 17x + 30$ **33.** $10x^2 + 5x - 5$

34. Summer Business Your weekly revenue R (in dollars) from your tie-dye T-shirt business can be modeled by

$R = -2t^2 + 88t + 90$

where t represents the number of weeks since the first week you started selling T-shirts. After how many weeks is the revenue $0?

35. Cliff Diving A cliff diver jumps from a ledge 96 feet above the ocean with an initial upward velocity of 16 feet per second. How long will it take until the diver enters the water?

36. Wall Mirror You plan on making a wall hanging that contains two small mirrors as shown.

a. Write a polynomial that represents the area of the wall hanging.

b. The area of the wall hanging will be 480 square inches. Find the length and width of the mirrors you will use.

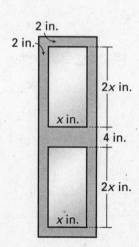

Copyright © by McDougal Littell, a division of Houghton Mifflin Company.

Practice
For use with pages 573–578

Factor the polynomial.

1. $x^2 - 36$

2. $25p^2 - 144$

3. $4b^2 - 100$

4. $36m^2 - 81$

5. $-2x^2 + 32$

6. $-4r^2 + 100s^2$

7. $y^2 + 24y + 144$

8. $9c^2 + 24c + 16$

9. $25w^2 - 20w + 4$

10. $16n^2 - 56n + 49$

11. $-18a^2 - 12a - 2$

12. $20z^2 - 140z + 245$

13. What is the factored form of $9a^2 - b^2$?

    A $(3a - b)^2$ **B** $(3a + b)^2$ **C** $(9a - b)^2$ **D** $(3a - b)(3a + b)$

Solve the equation.

14. $x^2 + 14x + 49 = 0$

15. $8w^2 = 50$

16. $64p^2 - 16p + 1 = 0$

17. $8a^2 - 72 = 0$

18. $3m^2 + 30m + 75 = 0$

19. $-4y^2 + 32y - 64 = 0$

20. $-5x^2 + 125 = 0$

21. $-7r^2 + 140r = 700$

22. $24w^2 + 6 = 24w$

23. $18n^2 + 60n + 50 = 0$

24. $\frac{25}{2}x^2 + 15x + \frac{9}{2} = 0$

25. $4x^2 = \frac{9}{16}$

LESSON 9.8 **Practice** *continued*
For use with pages 573–578

Find the roots of the polynomial.

26. $25m^2 - 289$ **27.** $7p^2 - 343$ **28.** $-3g^2 - 54g - 243$

29. **Measuring Tape** A measuring tape drops from a roof that is 16 feet above the ground. After how many seconds does the measuring tape land on the ground?

30. **Playground** A curved ladder that children can climb on can be modeled by the equation

$$y = -\frac{1}{20}x^2 + x$$

where x and y are measured in feet.

a. Make a table of values that shows the height of the ladder for $x = 0, 4, 8, 12,$ and 16 feet from the left end.

b. For what additional values of x does the equation make sense? *Explain.*

c. Use your table from part (a) to approximate the distance from the left end at which the arch reaches a height of 5 feet. Check your answer algebraically.

Practice
For use with pages 579–586

CA Standards
Alg. 11.0
Alg. 14.0
Alg. 25.1

Factor the expression.

1. $4x(x + 5) - 3(x + 5)$

2. $12(a - 3) - 2a(a - 3)$

3. $w^2(w + 8) - 5(w + 8)$

4. $2b^2(b + 6) + 3(b + 6)$

5. $y(15 + x) - (x + 15)$

6. $3x(4 + y) - 6(4 + y)$

Factor the polynomial by grouping.

7. $x^3 + x^2 + 5x + 5$

8. $y^3 - 14y^2 + y - 14$

9. $m^3 - 6m^2 + 2m - 12$

10. $p^3 + 9p^2 + 4p + 36$

11. $t^3 + 12t^2 - 2t - 24$

12. $3n^3 - 3n^2 + n - 1$

Factor the polynomial completely.

13. $7x^3 + 28x^2$

14. $4m^3 - 16m$

15. $-16p^3 - 2p$

16. $48r^3 - 30r^2$

17. $15y - 60y^2$

18. $18xy - 24x^2$

19. $5m^2 + 20m + 40$

20. $6x^2 + 6x - 120$

21. $4z^3 - 4z^2 - 8z$

22. $9x^3 + 36x^2 + 36$

23. $x^3 + x^2 + 4x + 4$

24. $d^3 + 4d^2 + 5d + 20$

Practice *continued*
For use with pages 579–586

Solve the equation.

25. $3x^2 + 18x + 24 = 0$ **26.** $10x^2 = 250$ **27.** $4m^2 - 28m + 49 = 0$

28. $12x^2 + 18x + 6 = 0$ **29.** $18x^2 - 48x + 32 = 0$ **30.** $-18x^2 - 60x - 50 = 0$

Find the roots of the polynomial.

31. $c^3 - 3c^2 - 4c + 12$ **32.** $2w^3 + 4w^2 - 30w$ **33.** $-5x^3 + 45x$

34. **Countertop** A countertop will have a hole drilled in it to hold
a cylindrical container that will function as a utensil holder.
The area of the entire countertop is given by $5x^2 + 12x + 7$.
The area of the hole is given by $x^2 + 2x + 1$. Write an
expression for the area in factored form of the countertop
that is left after the hole is drilled.

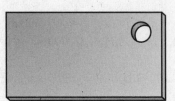

35. **Film Canister** A film canister in the shape of a cylinder has
a height of 8 centimeters and a volume of 32π cubic centimeters.
Write and solve an equation to find the radius of the film canister.

36. **Badminton** You hit a badminton birdie upward with a racket from
a height of 4 feet with an initial velocity of 12 feet per second.

a. Write an equation that models this situation.

b. How high is the birdie at 0.1 second?

c. How high is the birdie at 0.25 second?

d. How long will it take the birdie to reach the ground?

LESSON 10.1 **Practice**
For use with pages 605–611

Use the quadratic function to complete the table of values.

1. $y = 9x^2$

x	−2	−1	0	1	2
y	?	?	?	?	?

2. $y = -5x^2$

x	−2	−1	0	1	2
y	?	?	?	?	?

3. $y = \frac{5}{2}x^2 + 1$

x	−4	−2	0	2	4
y	?	?	?	?	?

4. $y = -\frac{1}{8}x^2 - 2$

x	−16	−8	0	8	16
y	?	?	?	?	?

5. $y = -4x^2 + 3$

x	−2	−1	0	1	2
y	?	?	?	?	?

6. $y = 6x^2 - 5$

x	−2	−1	0	1	2
y	?	?	?	?	?

Match the function with its graph.

7. $y = -4x^2 + 3$

8. $y = 3x^2 + 4$

9. $y = \frac{1}{3}x^2 - 4$

10. $y = \frac{1}{4}x^2 - 3$

11. $y = -3x^2 + 4$

12. $y = 4x^2 + 3$

A.

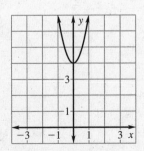

B.

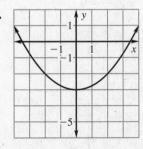

C.

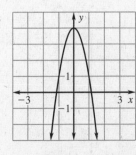

LESSON 10.1 **Practice** *continued*
For use with pages 605–611

D.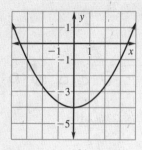

E.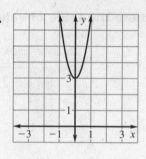

F.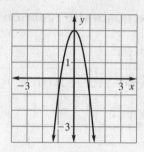

Describe how you can use the graph of $y = x^2$ to graph the given function.

13. $y = x^2 - 8$

14. $y = -x^2 + 4$

15. $y = 2x^2 + 3$

16. $y = -5x^2 + 1$

17. $y = \frac{1}{2}x^2 - 2$

18. $y = -\frac{3}{4}x^2 + 5$

Graph the function and identify its domain and range. Compare the graph with the graph of $y = x^2$.

19. $y = x^2 + 9$

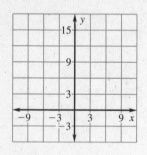

20. $y = -\frac{1}{5}x^2$

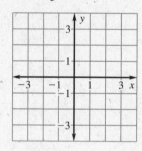

21. $y = -\frac{3}{2}x^2$

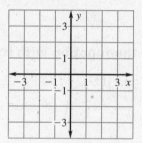

22. $y = x^2 - 3.5$

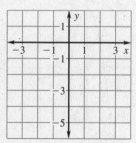

23. $y = 2x^2 - 9$

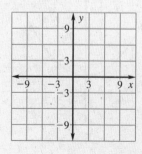

24. $y = -5x^2 + 2$

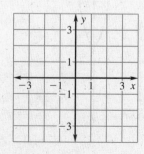

LESSON 10.1 **Practice** *continued*
For use with pages 605–611

25. Serving Plate The top view of a freeform serving plate you made in
a ceramics class is shown in the graph. One edge of the plate can be
modeled by the graph of the function $y = -\frac{5}{81}x^2 + 20$ where x and y
are measured in inches.

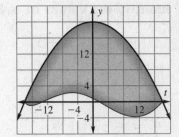

a. Find the domain of the function in this situation.

b. Find the range of the function in this situation.

26. Roof Shingle A roof shingle is dropped from a rooftop that is
100 feet above the ground. The height y (in feet) of the dropped
roof shingle is given by the function $y = -16t^2 + 100$ where t
is the time (in seconds) since the shingle is dropped.

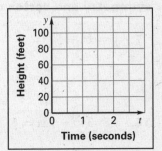

a. Graph the function.

b. Identify the domain and range of the function in this situation.

c. Use the graph to estimate the shingle's height at 1 second.

d. Use the graph to estimate when the shingle is at a height of 50 feet.

e. Use the graph to estimate when the shingle is at a height of 0 feet.

LESSON 10.1

LESSON 10.2 Practice
For use with pages 612–617

CA Standards
Alg. 21.0

Identify the values of *a*, *b*, and *c* in the quadratic function.

1. $y = 6x^2 + 3x + 5$

$a = 6 \cdot b = 3 \quad c = 5$

2. $y = \frac{3}{2}x^2 - x + 8$

$a = \frac{3}{2} \quad b = -1 \quad c = 8$

3. $y = 7x^2 - 3x - 1$

$a = 7 \quad b = -3 \quad c = -1$

4. $y = -2x^2 + 9x$

$a = -2 \quad b = 9$
$c = 0$

5. $y = \frac{3}{4}x^2 - 10$

$a = \frac{3}{4} \quad b = -10$
$c = 0$

6. $y = -8x^2 + 3x - 7$

$a = -8 \quad b = 3$
$c = -7$

Tell whether the graph opens upward or downward. Then find the axis of symmetry and vertex of the graph of the function.

$a = -2 \quad b = 4 \quad 6$

22.5
42.5
12.5
5.0
$a = 1$
$b = -5$

7. $y = x^2 - 5$ negative

$x = -\frac{-5}{2(a)} = \frac{5}{2} = \boxed{2.5 \text{ axis of sym}}$

$y = 2.5(2.5) - 5$
$62.5 - 5 \quad \boxed{y = 57.5, 25} \text{ vertex}$

$a = -1 \quad b = 9$

8. $y = -x^2 + 9$ positive

$x = -\frac{9}{2(-1)} = \boxed{4.5}$ vertex 4.5, 29.5

$y = -4.5(4.5) + 9$
$20.25 + 9 = 29.5$

9. $y = -2x^2 + 6x + 7$

$x = \frac{6}{-2(-2)} = \frac{6}{-4}$

22
61.5
4.5
1225.
180
2025

10. $y = 3x^2 - 12x + 1$

11. $y = 3x^2 + 6x - 2$

12. $y = -2x^2 + 7x - 21$

13. $y = \frac{1}{2}x^2 + 5x - 4$

14. $y = -\frac{1}{4}x^2 - 24$

15. $y = -3x^2 + 9x - 8$

16. $y = 3x^2 - 2x + 3$

17. $y = -2x^2 + 7x + 1$

18. $y = 3x^2 + 2x - 5$

Find the vertex of the graph of the function. Make a table of values using *x*-values to the left and right of the vertex.

19. $y = x^2 - 10x + 3$

x	?	?	?	?	?
y	?	?	?	?	?

20. $y = -x^2 + 6x - 2$

x	?	?	?	?	?
y	?	?	?	?	?

LESSON 10.2

Practice *continued*
For use with pages 612–617

21. $y = \frac{1}{2}x^2 - x + 7$

x	?	?	?	?	?
y	?	?	?	?	?

22. $y = \frac{1}{3}x^2 - 2x + 3$

x	?	?	?	?	?
y	?	?	?	?	?

Graph the function. Label the vertex and axis of symmetry.

23. $y = -x^2 - 10$

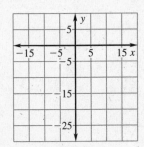

24. $y = 2x^2 + 3$

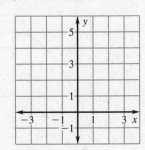

25. $y = -2x^2 + 2x + 1$

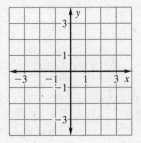

26. $y = 5x^2 + 2x$

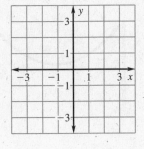

27. $y = -2x^2 + x - 4$

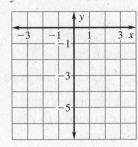

28. $y = x^2 - 8x + 5$

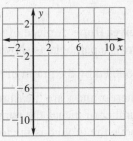

29. $y = -\frac{1}{2}x^2 - 8x + 3$

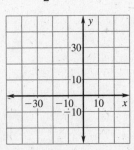

30. $y = \frac{1}{4}x^2 + 3x - 1$

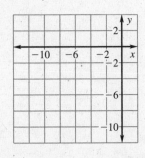

31. $y = -\frac{3}{4}x^2 - 2x + 2$

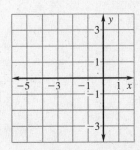

LESSON 10.2

Practice continued
For use with pages 612–617

Tell whether the function has a *minimum value* or a *maximum value*.
Then find the minimum or maximum value.

32. $y = 8x^2 - 40$ **33.** $y = -5x^2 + 10x - 2$ **34.** $y = 8x^2 - 4x + 4$

35. Storage Building The roof of the storage building shown can be modeled by the graph of the function $y = -0.12x^2 + 2.4x$ where x and y are measured in feet. What is the height h at the highest point of the building as shown in the diagram?

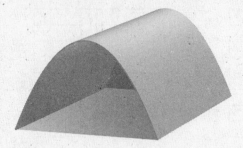
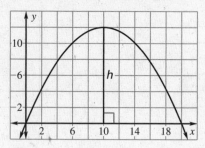

36. Velvet Rope A piece of velvet rope near a museum display forms a parabola as shown. This parabola can be modeled by the graph of the function $y = \dfrac{4}{225}x^2 - \dfrac{16}{15}x + 40$ where x and y are measured in inches and y represents the number of inches the parabola is above the ground. How far above the ground is the lowest point on the rope?

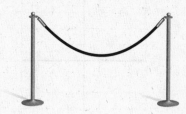

LESSON 10.3 **Practice**
For use with pages 618–623

Find the *x*-intercepts of the graph of the quadratic function.

1. $y = (x - 3)(x - 2)$

X = 3 X = 2
x intercepts

2. $y = (x + 4)(x + 7)$

X = -4 X = -7
x intercepts

3. $y = (x - 6)(x + 8)$

X = 6 X = -8
x - intercepts

4. $y = 3(x + 1)(x - 4)$

X = -1 X = 4
x - intercepts

5. $y = -5(x - 4)(x - 9)$

Y = 4 x = 9

6. $y = \frac{1}{2}(x - 2)(x + 11)$

X = 2 X = -11

7. $y = \frac{3}{4}(x + 8)(x + 12)$

X = -8 X = -12

8. $y = -\frac{17}{18}(x + 8)(x + 12)$

X = -8 X = -12

Graph the quadratic function. Label the vertex, axis of symmetry, and *x*-intercept(s).

9. $y = (x - 2)(x + 2)$

10. $y = (x + 2)(x - 4)$

11. $y = -(x + 1)(x - 3)$

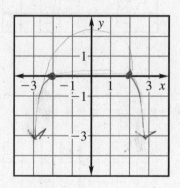
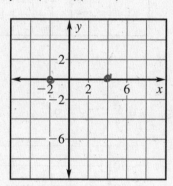
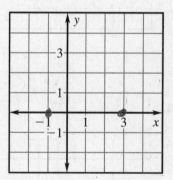

X - intercepts

X = -2 X = 2

axis of symmetry

X = $\frac{2 + (-2)}{2}$ = $\frac{0}{2}$ X = 0

LESSON 10.3

Practice *continued*

For use with pages 618–623

12. $y = 2(x - 5)(x + 1)$

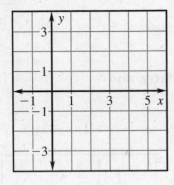

13. $y = -3(x - 2)(x - 6)$

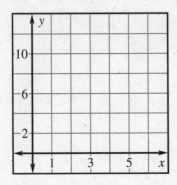

14. $y = \frac{1}{2}(x + 2)^2$

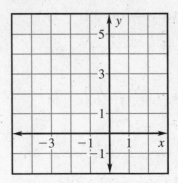

15. $y = -\frac{1}{4}(x - 2)^2$

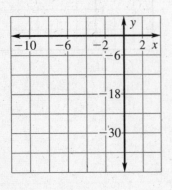

16. $y = x^2 + 2x - 24$

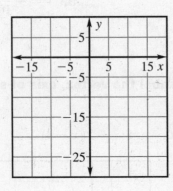

17. $y = 5x^2 + 30x + 45$

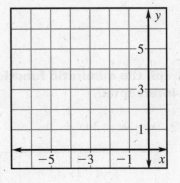

18. $y = x^2 + 6x - 27$

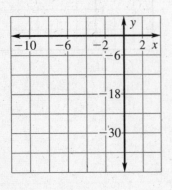

19. $y = \frac{x^2}{4} - 3x + 9$

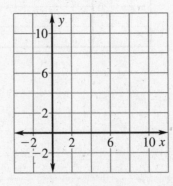

20. $y = \frac{x^2}{5} - \frac{x}{3} - 4$

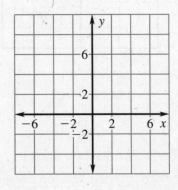

LESSON 10.3 **Practice** *continued*
For use with pages 618–623

Write a quadratic function in intercept form whose graph has the given x-intercept(s) and passes through the given point.

21. x-intercepts: -1 and 3
point: $(1, -8)$

22. x-intercepts: 2 and 4
point: $(3, -5)$

23. x-intercepts: -4 and 5
point: $(0, -10)$

24. x-intercepts: 1 and -10
point: $(2, -84)$

25. only x-intercept: 3
point: $(4, -6)$

26. only x-intercept: -4
point: $\left(0, \frac{16}{5}\right)$

27. **Golf** A golfer makes a chip shot onto the green. The ball takes a parabolic path through the air as shown. Write a function whose graph models the flight path of the ball.

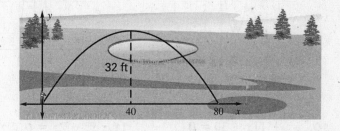

28. **Roof** A building has a parabolic roof as shown. Use the coordinate axes in the diagram to write a function whose graph models the parabolic shape of the roof.

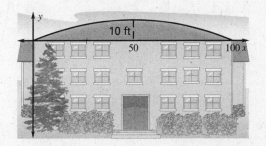

LESSON 10.4 Practice
For use with pages 624–631

CA Standards
Alg. 21.0

Determine whether the given value is a solution of the equation.

1. $x^2 - 2x + 15 = 0$; 3

2. $x^2 - 4x - 12 = 0$; 2

3. $-x^2 - 5x - 6 = 0$; 3

4. $x^2 + 3x - 4 = 0$; 1

5. $2x^2 + 9x - 5 = 0$; -2

6. $3x^2 - 5x - 2 = 0$; 2

Use the graph to find the solutions of the given equation.

7. $x^2 + 8x + 16 = 0$

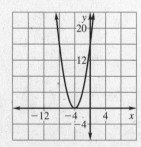

8. $-x^2 + 36 = 0$

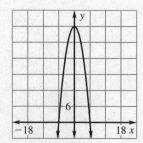

9. $x^2 + 5x - 24 = 0$

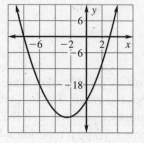

10. $x^2 + 11x + 30 = 0$

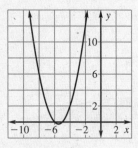

11. $x^2 - 25 = 0$

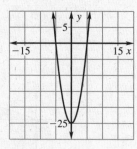

12. $x^2 + 7 = 0$

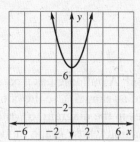

Solve the equation by graphing.

13. $-x^2 - 6x = 0$

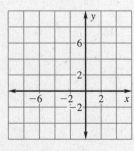

14. $2x^2 = 2$

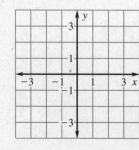

15. $x^2 - 7x + 10 = 0$

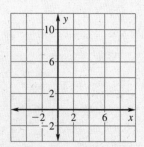

Name _____ Date _____

LESSON
10.4 **Practice** *continued*
For use with pages 624–631

16. $x^2 = 10x$

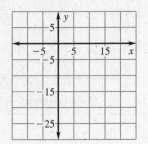

17. $x^2 - 6x + 9 = 0$

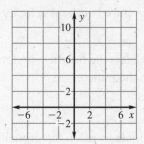

18. $-x^2 + 9x = 18$

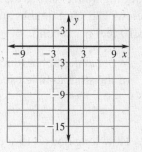

Approximate the zeros of the function to the nearest tenth.

19. $y = -x^2 - 2x + 2$

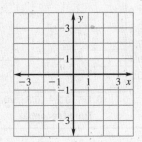

20. $y = x^2 - 5x + 3$

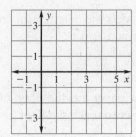

21. $y = 2x^2 - 3x - 1$

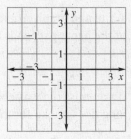

22. $y = x^2 + 2x - 1$

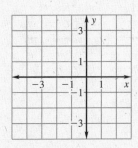

23. $y = -2x^2 + x + 4$

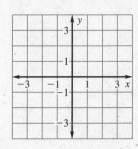

24. $y = \dfrac{x^2}{2} - 3x + 3$

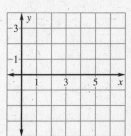

LESSON 10.4 **Practice** *continued*
For use with pages 624–631

25. Stunt Double A movie stunt double jumps from the top of a building 50 feet above the ground onto a pad on the ground below. The stunt double jumps with an initial vertical velocity of 10 feet per second.

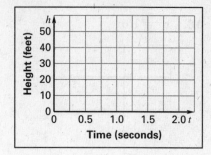

a. Write and graph a function that models the height h (in feet) of the stunt double t seconds after she jumps.

b. How long does it take the stunt double to reach the ground?

26. Wastebasket You throw a wad of used paper towards a wastebasket from a height of about 1.3 feet above the floor with an initial vertical velocity of 3 feet per second.

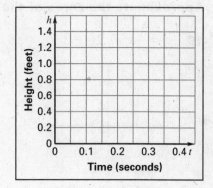

a. Write and graph a function that models the height h (in feet) of the paper t seconds after it is thrown.

b. If you miss the wastebasket and the paper hits the floor, how long does it take for the ball of paper to reach the floor?

c. If the ball of paper hits the rim of the wastebasket one-half foot above the ground, how long was the ball in the air?

LESSON 10.6 Practice
For use with pages 642–648

Find the value of *c* that makes the expression a perfect square trinomial. Then write the expression as a square of a binomial.

1. $x^2 + 12x + c$

2. $x^2 + 50x + c$

3. $x^2 - 26x + c$

4. $x^2 - 18x + c$

5. $x^2 + 13x + c$

6. $x^2 - 9x + c$

7. $x^2 - 11x + c$

8. $x^2 + \frac{1}{2}x + c$

9. $x^2 - \frac{6}{5}x + c$

Solve the equation by completing the square.

10. $x^2 + 6x = 1$

11. $x^2 + 4x = 13$

12. $x^2 - 10x = 15$

13. $x^2 + 8x = 10$

14. $x^2 - 2x - 7 = 0$

15. $x^2 - 12x - 21 = 0$

16. $x^2 + 3x - 2 = 0$

17. $x^2 + 5x - 3 = 0$

18. $x^2 - x = 1$

Find the value of *x*. Round your answer to the nearest hundredth, if necessary.

19. Area of triangle = 30 ft^2

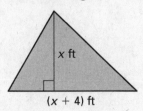

x ft

(x + 4) ft

20. Area of rectangle = 140 in.^{2}

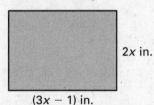

2x in.

(3x − 1) in.

LESSON 10.6

21. **Colorado** The state of Colorado is almost perfectly rectangular, with its north
border 111 miles longer than its west border. If the state encompasses
104,000 square miles, estimate the dimensions of Colorado. Round your
answer to the nearest mile.

22. **Baseball** After a baseball is hit, the height h (in feet) of the ball above the ground
t seconds after it is hit can be approximated by the equation $h = -16t^2 + 65t + 3$.
Determine how long it will take for the ball to hit the ground. Round your answer
to the nearest hundredth.

23. **Fenced-In Yard** You have 60 feet of fencing to fence in part of
your backyard for your dog. You want to make sure that your dog
has 400 square feet of space to run around in. The back of your
house will be used as one side of the enclosure as shown.

a. Write equations for the perimeter and area of the enclosure.

b. Use substitution to solve the system of equations from part (a).
What are the possible lengths and widths of the enclosure?

LESSON 10.7

Practice
For use with pages 649–655

Use the quadratic formula to find the roots of the polynomial.

1. $x^2 + 7x - 80$

2. $3x^2 - x - 16$

3. $8x^2 - 2x - 30$

4. $x^2 + 4x + 1$

Use the quadratic formula to solve the equation. Round your solutions to the nearest hundredth, if necessary.

5. $-x^2 + x + 12 = 0$

6. $-3x^2 - 4x + 10 = 0$

7. $5x^2 + 30x + 32 = 0$

8. $x^2 + 6x - 100 = 0$

9. $4x^2 - x - 20 = 0$

10. $5x^2 + x - 9 = 0$

11. $6x^2 + 7x - 3 = 0$

12. $10x^2 - 7x + 5 = 0$

Tell which method(s) you would use to solve the quadratic equation. *Explain* your choice(s).

13. $6x^2 - 216 = 0$

14. $8x^2 = 56$

15. $5x^2 - 10x = 0$

16. $x^2 + 8x + 7 = 0$

17. $x^2 - 6x + 1 = 0$

18. $-9x^2 + 10x = 5$

LESSON 10.7

Practice *continued*
For use with pages 649–655

**Solve the quadratic equation using any method. Round your solutions
to the nearest hundredth, if necessary.**

19. $-10x^2 = -50$ **20.** $x^2 - 16x = -64$ **21.** $x^2 + 3x - 8 = 0$

22. $x^2 = 14x - 49$ **23.** $x^2 + 6x = 14$ **24.** $-5x^2 + x = 13$

25. Pasta For the period 1990–2003, the amount of biscuits, pasta, and noodles y
(in thousands of metric tons) imported into the United States can be modeled by
the function $y = 1.36x^2 + 27.8x + 304$ where x is the number of years since 1990.

a. Write and solve an equation that you can use to approximate the year in which
500 million pounds of biscuits, pasta, and noodles were imported.

b. Write and solve an equation that you can use to approximate the year in which
575 million pounds of biscuits, pasta, and noodles were imported.

26. Eggs For the period 1997–2003, the number of eggs y (in billions) produced in
the United States can be modeled by the function $y = -0.27x^2 + 3.3x + 77$ where
x is the number of years since 1997.

a. Write and solve an equation that you can use to approximate the year(s) in which
80 billion eggs were produced.

b. Check the reasonableness of your answer in part (a) by substituting it back into
the equation.

LESSON
10.8 **Practice**
For use with pages 656–662

CA Standards
Alg. 20.0
Alg. 22.0

Tell whether the equation has *two solutions, one solution,* or *no solution*.

1. $x^2 + x + 3 = 0$

2. $2x^2 - 4x - 5 = 0$

3. $-2x^2 + 10x - 5 = 0$

4. $3x^2 - 9x + 8 = 0$

5. $10x^2 - 8x + 1 = 0$

6. $-4x^2 + 9 = 0$

7. $36x^2 - 9x = 0$

8. $3x^2 + 2 = 4x$

9. $12 = x^2 - 6x$

10. $\frac{1}{6}x^2 + 3 = x$

11. $-8x^2 - 9x = \frac{2}{3}$

12. $8x^2 + 12x + 2 = 4x$

Find the number of *x*-intercepts of the graph by using the discriminant.

13. $y = x^2 - 6x - 3$

14. $y = 5x^2 - x - 1$

15. $y = 6x^2 - 6x + 1$

16. $y = x^2 + x + 6$

17. $y = -4x^2 + x + 1$

18. $y = 4x^2 + 5x - 1$

19. $y = 2x^2 - 4x + 2$

20. $y = 10x^2 - 5x + 1$

21. $y = 8x^2 + x + 4$

22. $y = -15x^2 + 3x + 5$

23. $y = \frac{1}{2}x^2 - 4x + 8$

24. $y = \frac{2}{3}x^2 - 5x + 2$

LESSON 10.8 **Practice** *continued*
For use with pages 656–662

Give a value of c for which the equation has (a) two solutions, (b) one solution, and (c) no solution.

25. $x^2 + 10x + c = 0$ **26.** $x^2 - 4x + c = 0$ **27.** $25x^2 + 10x + c = 0$

28. $49x^2 - 14x + c = 0$ **29.** $2x^2 + 4x + c = 0$ **30.** $3x^2 - 18x + c = 0$

31. Playhouse You want to build a playhouse for your sister in your backyard. You have blueprints which show that the playhouse is 12 feet long and 13 feet wide. You want to change the dimensions as shown. The new area of the front of the house can be modeled by the function $y = -x^2 + x + 156$.

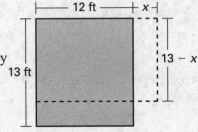

a. Write an equation that you can use to determine if there is a value of x that gives an area of 150 square feet.

b. Use the discriminant of your equation from part (a) to show that it is possible to find a value of x for which the area is 150 square feet.

c. Find the value(s) of x for which the area is 150 square feet.

32. Tennis You and your friend are walking around the exterior of a tennis court that has a 12-foot high fence around it. You pick up a ball and try to throw it from a height of 5 feet over the fence. You throw it with an initial vertical velocity of 20 feet per second. Can the ball make it over the fence?

Practice
For use with pages 679–687

Tell whether the equation represents *direct variation*, *inverse variation*, or *neither*.

1. $y = -11x$

2. $xy = -5$

3. $y = x - 4$

4. $x = \dfrac{-8}{y}$

5. $xy = 14$

6. $\dfrac{y}{x} = 13$

7. $2x + y = 8$

8. $3y = \dfrac{9}{x}$

9. $4x - 4y = 0$

Graph the inverse variation equation.

10. $xy = 12$

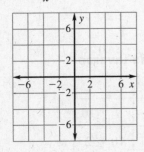

11. $xy = -6$

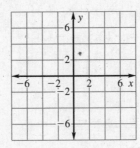

12. $xy = 7$

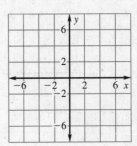

13. $y = \dfrac{-8}{x}$

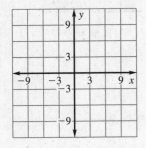

14. $y = \dfrac{15}{x}$

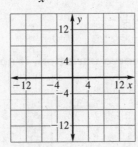

15. $y = \dfrac{14}{x}$

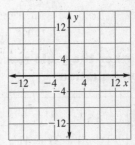

<table>
<tr><td>LESSON
11.1</td><td>Practice continued
For use with pages 679–687</td></tr>
</table>

16. $y = \dfrac{-9}{x}$

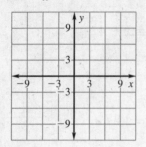

17. $y = \dfrac{-12}{x}$

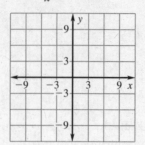

18. $y = \dfrac{5}{x}$

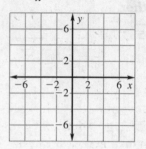

Given that y varies inversely with x, use the specified values to write an inverse variation equation that relates x and y. Then find the value of y when $x = 2$.

19. $x = 7, y = 2$

20. $x = 3, y = 9$

21. $x = -3, y = 1$

22. $x = 11, y = -1$

23. $x = -12, y = -12$

24. $x = -18, y = -4$

25. $x = 10, y = 5$

26. $x = 7, y = -4$

27. $x = 6, y = 6$

28. $x = -3, y = 12$

29. $x = -5, y = 40$

30. $x = -5, y = -11$

Tell whether the table represents inverse variation. If so, write the inverse variation equation.

31.

x	2	4	6	8	10
y	11	21	31	41	51

32.

x	−5	−4	1	2	10
y	−4	−5	20	10	2

LESSON 11.1

LESSON
11.2

Practice *continued*
For use with pages 688–695

19. **Zoo Exhibit** The directors of a zoo have drawn up preliminary plans for a rectangular exhibit. They have decided on dimensions that are related as shown.

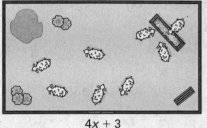

$4x - 2$

$4x + 3$

    a. Write a rational expression for the ratio of the perimeter to the area of the exhibit.

    b. Simplify your expression from part (a).

20. **Materials Used** The material consumed M (in thousands of pounds) by a plastic injection molding machine per year between 1995 and 2004 can be modeled by

$$M = \frac{8t^2 + 66t + 70}{(3 - 0.2t + 0.1t^2)(t + 7)}$$

where t is the number of years since 1995. Simplify the model and approximate the number of pounds consumed in 2000.

LESSON 11.3 **Practice**
For use with pages 696–703

Find the product.

1. $\dfrac{4x^2}{15} \cdot \dfrac{5}{8x^5}$ $\boxed{\dfrac{20x^2}{120x^5}}$

2. $\dfrac{24}{7x^2} \cdot \dfrac{14x^6}{40}$ $\boxed{\dfrac{336x^6}{280x^2}}$

3. $\dfrac{21}{2x + 12} \cdot \dfrac{4x + 24}{15}$ $= \dfrac{21(4x+24}{15(2x+12)}$

$\dfrac{84x + 504}{30x + 180}$ $= \dfrac{4 \cdot 2 \cdot 2 + 7 \cdot 3 \cdot 2}{5 \cdot 3 \cdot 2 + 5 \cdot 3 \cdot 2}$

$\boxed{\dfrac{84}{30}}$

4. $\dfrac{5x + 10}{2x - 6} \cdot \dfrac{x - 3}{10x + 20}$

5. $\dfrac{x - 3}{2x + 8} \cdot \dfrac{x + 4}{x^2 + 2x - 15}$

6. $\dfrac{x^2 + 4x - 12}{x^2 + 7x + 10} \cdot \dfrac{x + 5}{2x - 4}$

7. $\dfrac{6x}{4x^2 - 1} \cdot \dfrac{2x^2 + 7x + 3}{18}$

8. $\dfrac{x^4}{x^4 + 5x^3} \cdot (x + 5)$

9. $\dfrac{3x - 6}{x^2 - x - 2} \cdot (x^2 + 6x + 5)$

Find the quotient.

10. $\dfrac{24}{5x^3} \div \dfrac{6}{25x^2}$ $\boxed{\dfrac{4}{5x}}$

11. $\dfrac{11x^4}{18} \div \dfrac{22}{9x^2}$ $= \boxed{\dfrac{2x^4}{2x^2}}$

12. $\dfrac{7x + 21}{30} \div \dfrac{21x + 63}{20}$ $\dfrac{(7x+21) \div (21x+63)}{30 \div 20}$

$\boxed{\dfrac{3x + 3}{10}}$

13. $\dfrac{4x - 24}{3x + 15} \div \dfrac{12x - 72}{x + 5}$ $= \boxed{\dfrac{3x - 3}{3x + 3}}$

14. $\dfrac{x + 2}{3x - 3} \div \dfrac{x^2 + 11x + 18}{x - 1}$ $= \dfrac{(x+2)(x+9)(x+2)}{(3x-3)(x-1)}$

$\boxed{\dfrac{x + 9}{x - 1}}$

15. $\dfrac{x^2 + 4x}{4x} \div \dfrac{x^2 + x - 12}{x - 3}$

16. $\dfrac{2x + 10}{x^2 - 25} \div \dfrac{4x^2}{2x^2 - 10x}$

17. $\dfrac{2x - 14}{x^2 - 4x - 21} \div (x + 3)$

Practice *continued*
For use with pages 705–712

19. $\dfrac{x+3}{x-1} + \dfrac{x+2}{x+1}$

20. $\dfrac{2x}{x^2-3x} + \dfrac{x+4}{x-3}$

21. $\dfrac{1}{x^2+5x+4} - \dfrac{1}{x^2-16}$

22. Paddle Boat You paddle boat 8 miles upstream (against the current) and 8 miles downstream (with the current). The speed of the current is 1 mile per hour.

   a. Write an equation that gives the total travel time t (in hours) as a function of your average speed r (in miles per hour) in still water.

   b. Find your total travel time if your average speed in still water is 3 miles per hour.

   c. How much faster is your total travel time if you increased your average speed in still water to 3.5 miles per hour? Round your answer to the nearest tenth.

23. Bike Ride You bike 50 miles from home. On your way back home, your average speed increases by 3 miles per hour.

   a. Write an equation that gives the total biking time t (in hours) as a function of your average speed r (in miles per hour) when you are biking away from home.

   b. Find the total biking time if you bike away from your home at an average speed of 15 miles per hour. Round your answer to the nearest tenth.

   c. How much longer is your total biking time if you bike away from your home at an average speed of 12 miles per hour?

Solve the equation. Check your solution.

1. $\dfrac{x}{27} = \dfrac{3}{x}$ $x^2 = 81$
   $\boxed{x = 9}$

$\begin{array}{r} 227 \\ \times\ 3 \\ \hline 81 \end{array}$

2. $\dfrac{3}{x} = \dfrac{2}{x+4}$ $3(x+4) = 2(x)$
   $3x + 12 = 2x$
   $\underline{-3x \qquad -3x}$

3. $\dfrac{4}{x-7} = \dfrac{2}{x}$

4. $\dfrac{10}{x+2} = \dfrac{7}{x-4}$

5. $\dfrac{-5}{x+4} = \dfrac{x}{x+4}$

6. $\dfrac{8}{x+8} = \dfrac{x}{x+2}$

7. $\dfrac{-1}{x+2} = \dfrac{x}{x+2}$

8. $\dfrac{2}{3x} = \dfrac{x+3}{2x-5}$

9. $\dfrac{6x}{x+2} = \dfrac{-2}{x+2}$

Find the LCD of the rational expressions in the equation.

10. $\dfrac{7x}{x-3} + 4 = \dfrac{x+1}{x-3}$

11. $\dfrac{3}{2x-2} + 4 = \dfrac{7x}{x-1}$

12. $\dfrac{7}{x-2} + 1 = \dfrac{4}{x-3}$

Solve the equation. Check your solution.

13. $\dfrac{3x}{x+4} - 3 = \dfrac{-12}{x+4}$

14. $\dfrac{3}{x+2} + 5 = \dfrac{4}{x+2}$

15. $\dfrac{2x}{x-1} + 2 = \dfrac{10}{x+2}$

16. $\dfrac{x-1}{x+5} + 6 = \dfrac{-2}{x+2}$

17. $\dfrac{4x}{x-5} + 1 = \dfrac{9}{x-1}$

18. $\dfrac{x}{x-4} - \dfrac{5x}{x-2} = \dfrac{-18}{x-2}$

Practice *continued*
For use with pages 713–718

19. Stain Mixing You are staining a coffee table you just made. After testing some sample pieces of wood, you decide that you want a mix of a yellow stain and a red stain. You estimate that you want a mix that contains 75% of the yellow stain. You only have 1 pint that is made up of equal parts of the stain. How many pints of the yellow stain do you have to add to the current mixture?

20. Batting Average In baseball, a player's batting average (in decimal form) is the total number of hits divided by the total number of at-bats. Suppose a player has 47 hits in 166 at-bats. How many consecutive hits does the player need to raise his batting average to 0.320?

21. Motorcycles Some motorcycles have two-stroke engines that require a gas and oil mixture in order to run properly. A common ratio for the gas to oil mixture is 32 parts gas to 1 part oil. Suppose 5 gallons of gas already have 8 ounces of oil mixed in. How many more ounces of oil need to be added to get the proper mixture?
(1 gal = 128 oz)

LESSON 11.6 Practice
For use with pages 721–725

CA Standards
Alg. 15.0

Express the work rate as a fraction of the job per hour.

1. Todd can trim the bushes in 2 hours.

2. Jenelle can clean her house in 5 hours.

3. Luis can build a shed in 7 hours 30 minutes.

Find the part of the job the person can complete in t minutes.

4. Alexis reads an article in 9 minutes.

5. Pat finishes a cross-country race in 24 minutes.

6. Sara varnishes the bookcase in 1 hour 15 minutes.

LESSON 11.6

LESSON 11.6

Practice *continued*
For use with pages 721–725

7. **Wallpaper** Working together, an expert wallpaper hanger and an assistant can hang the wallpaper in a room in 3 hours. The assistant can hang the wallpaper in twice the amount of time it takes the expert wallpaper hanger to hang the wallpaper alone. Let x represent the time (in hours) that the assistant can hang the wallpaper alone.

   a. Copy and complete the table below.

Person	Fraction of room papered each hour	Time (hours)	Fraction of room papered
Assistant	$\frac{1}{x}$	3	?
Expert	?	3	?

   b. *Explain* why the sum of the expressions in the last column must be 1.

   c. Write a rational equation that you can use to find the amount of time it takes the assistant to wallpaper the room alone. Then solve the equation.

8. **Garage** Richie can build a small garage in 50 hours. Pedro can build the same garage in 30 hours. How long will it take Richie and Pedro to build the garage if they work together?

9. **Computer Project** Macy and Rachel can complete their computer project in 4 hours working together. Macy would take 6 hours to complete the project on her own. How long would Rachel take to complete the project on her own?

LESSON 11.6

LESSON 12.1 Practice
For use with pages 743–749

CA Standards
Gr. 6 SDAP 3.0

Find the number of possible outcomes in the sample space. Then list the possible outcomes.

1. A bag contains 6 blue cards numbered 1–6 and 8 red cards numbered 1–8. You choose a card at random.

2. You choose one out of four numbers and toss two coins.

3. You roll two 6-sided number cubes.

In Exercises 4–7, refer to the spinner shown. The spinner is divided into sections with the same area.

4. What is the probability that the spinner stops on an even number?

5. What is the probability that the spinner stops on an odd number?

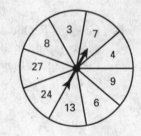

6. You spin the spinner 24 times. It stops on 27 twice. What is the experimental probability of stopping on 27?

7. You spin the spinner 30 times. It stops on a multiple of 3 five times. What is the experimental probability of stopping on a multiple of 3?

LESSON 12.1

Practice *continued*
For use with pages 743–749

8. **Favorite Spectator Sport** A survey asked a total of 180 students in your school about their favorite spectator sports. The table shows the results of the survey.

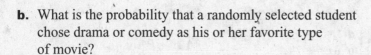

Sport	Basketball	Soccer	Football	Baseball	Volleyball	Wrestling	Hockey
Number of students	40	20	45	20	16	18	21

   a. What is the probability that a randomly selected student who participated in this survey chose football as his or her favorite spectator sport?

   b. What is the probability that a randomly selected student who participated in this survey chose wrestling or hockey as his or her favorite spectator sport?

9. **Movies** A local movie theater did a survey of students to determine their favorite types of movies. The circle graph shows the results of the survey.

   a. What is the probability that a randomly selected student chose science fiction as his or her favorite type of movie?

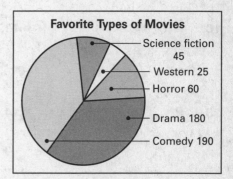

Favorite Types of Movies
- Science fiction 45
- Western 25
- Horror 60
- Drama 180
- Comedy 190

   b. What is the probability that a randomly selected student chose drama or comedy as his or her favorite type of movie?

LESSON 12.1

LESSON 12.2

LESSON 12.2 **Practice**
For use with pages 750–755

CA Standards
Alg. 2 18.0
Alg. 2 19.0

Find the number of ways you can arrange (a) all of the letters in the given word and (b) 2 of the letters in the word.

1. TACK

2. MAR

3. GAMER

Write the meaning of the notation in words.

4. $_{14}P_3$

5. $_{24}P_{10}$

6. $_{30}P_{20}$

Evaluate the expression.

7. $6!$

8. $9!$

9. $11!$

10. $\dfrac{8!}{3!}$

11. $\dfrac{12!}{9!}$

12. $\dfrac{15!}{14!}$

13. $_6P_3$

14. $_4P_4$

15. $_{15}P_3$

16. $_8P_7$

17. $_{10}P_6$

18. $_5P_0$

Complete the statement using >, <, or =.

19. $_6P_4 \underline{\ \ ?\ \ } _4P_1$

20. $_8P_6 \underline{\ \ ?\ \ } _{10}P_8$

21. $_3P_0 \underline{\ \ ?\ \ } _6P_5$

22. $_6P_3 \underline{\ \ ?\ \ } _4P_1$

23. $_{24}P_1 \underline{\ \ ?\ \ } _4P_4$

24. $_7P_5 \underline{\ \ ?\ \ } _{12}P_3$

Practice *continued*
For use with pages 750–755

25. Summer Reading List At the beginning of the summer, you have 6 books to read. In how many orders can you read the books?

26. Air Conditioning Repair An air conditioner repair person has repairs to make at 7 different homes. The destinations are all so close, it doesn't matter the order in which the repairs are made. In how many orders can the repairs be made?

27. Boat Racing You are in a boat racing competition. In each heat, 4 boats race and the positions of the boats are randomly assigned.

 a. In how many ways can a position be assigned?

 b. What is the probability that you are chosen to be in the last position? *Explain* how you found your answer.

 c. What is the probability that you are chosen to be in the first or second position of the heat that you are racing in? *Explain* how you found your answer.

 d. What is the probability that you are chosen to be in the second or third position of the heat that you are racing in? *Compare* your answer with that in part (c).

28. Math Exam On an exam, you are asked to list the 6 steps to solving a particular kind of problem in order. You guess the order of the steps at random. What is the probability that you choose the correct order?

LESSON 12.3 **Practice**
For use with pages 756–761

CA Standards
Alg. 2 18.0
Alg. 2 19.0

Evaluate the expression.

1. $_8C_4$

2. $_5C_5$

3. $_{12}C_0$

4. $_7C_1$

5. $_{15}C_{11}$

6. $_{10}C_3$

7. $_6C_5$

8. $_4C_2$

9. $_{16}C_8$

Complete the statement using >, <, or =.

10. $_{10}C_6 \underline{\ ?\ } {_8}C_5$

11. $_{22}C_3 \underline{\ ?\ } {_{18}}C_4$

12. $_9C_6 \underline{\ ?\ } {_9}C_3$

13. $_8C_2 \underline{\ ?\ } {_{15}}C_{14}$

14. $_7C_7 \underline{\ ?\ } {_{14}}C_{14}$

15. $_5C_3 \underline{\ ?\ } {_8}C_3$

In Exercises 16–18, tell whether the question can be answered using
combinations **or** *permutations.* *Explain* **your choice, then answer**
the question.

16. Five students from the 90 students in your class not running for class president
will be selected to count the ballots for the vote for class president. In how many
ways can the 5 students be selected?

17. Twenty students are running for 3 different positions on student council. In how
many ways can the 3 positions be filled?

18. To complete a quiz, you must answer 3 questions from a list of 6 questions.
In how many ways can you complete the quiz?

LESSON 12.3

LESSON 12.3 **Practice** *continued*
For use with pages 756–761

19. Sweaters The buyer for a retail store must decide which sweaters to stock for the upcoming fall season. A sweater from one manufacturer comes in 5 different colors and 3 different textures. The buyer decides that the store will stock the sweater in 3 different colors and 2 different textures. How many different sweaters are possible?

20. Greeting Cards A greeting card company packages 4 different cards together that are randomly selected from 10 different cards with a different animal on each card. What is the probability that one of the cards in a package is the card that has a dog on it?

21. Open-Mike Night A coffee shop offers an open-mike night for poetry. Tonight, 15 people would like to read, but there is only enough time to have 7 people read.

a. Seven of the 15 people that would like to read are randomly chosen. How many combinations of 7 readers from the group of people that would like to read are possible?

b. You and your friend are part of the group that would like to read. What is the probability that you and your friend are chosen? What is the probability that you are chosen first and your friend is chosen second? Which event is more likely to occur?

Name _____   Date _____

Practice
For use with pages 762–768

CA Standards
Gr. 6 SDAP 3.4
Gr. 6 SDAP 3.5

In Exercises 1–4, you draw a card from a bag that contains 4 yellow cards numbered 1–4 and 5 blue cards numbered 1–5. Tell whether the events A *and* B are *mutually exclusive* or *overlapping*. Then find P(A *or* B).

1. **Event A:** You choose a card with an even number.
   Event B: You choose a number 4 card.

2. **Event A:** You choose a yellow card.
   Event B: You choose a number 5 card.

3. **Event A:** You choose a blue number 3 card.
   Event B: You choose a blue card.

4. **Event A:** You choose a card with an odd number.
   Event B: You choose a blue card.

In Exercises 5 and 6, tell whether the events A *and* B are *dependent* or *independent*. Then find P(A *and* B).

5. A bag contains 6 red balls and 5 green balls. You randomly draw one ball, replace it, and randomly draw a second ball.
   Event A: The first ball is green.
   Event B: The second ball is green.

6. You write each of the letters of the word BRILLIANT on pieces of paper and place them in a bag. You randomly draw one letter, do not replace it, then randomly draw a second letter.
   Event A: The first letter is an L.
   Event B: The second letter is a T.

LESSON 12.4 **Practice** *continued*
For use with pages 762–768

7. **Eating Habits** A survey of 500 students in a school found that about 100 households consist of only vegetarians, 240 consist of vegetarians and non-vegetarians, and 160 consist of non-vegetarians.

   a. What is the probability that one of the households surveyed, chosen at random, consists of vegetarians or non-vegetarians?

   b. What is the probability that one of the households surveyed, chosen at random, consists of vegetarians and non-vegetarians?

   c. *Explain* how your answers to parts (a) and (b) are related.

8. **Coordinating Time** You study with a group for an upcoming math competition on Mondays, Tuesdays, and Thursdays. You volunteer at a hospital on Mondays, Wednesdays, and Thursdays.

   a. Make a Venn diagram that shows the days of the week that you participate in each activity.

   b. Your class is taking a field trip that could be scheduled for any day of the week (Monday through Friday). Find the probability that it is scheduled for a day when you are studying with your group or are volunteering.